EMILE GALLÉ

EMILE GALLÉ

DREAMS INTO GLASS

William Warmus

THE CORNING MUSEUM OF GLASS
CORNING, NEW YORK

Emile Gallé
Dreams into Glass
A special exhibition
The Corning Museum of Glass
Corning, New York
April 28 – October 21, 1984

Cover: Dragonfly Coupe. Nancy, France, 1903. Emile Gallé.
The Corning Museum of Glass and private collection. See 23.

Inside covers: Details from Gallé cabinet at Musée des
Techniques, Conservatoire des Arts et Métiers, Paris

Back: Mushroom Lamp. Nancy, France, about 1902, Emile Gallé.
Collection of Joanna Walker. See 30.

Printed in U.S.A.
Standard Book Number ISBN 0-87290-109-2
Library of Congress Catalog Number 83-073384

Design and Art Direction: Avanti Studio
Typography: Finn Typographic Service, Inc.
Printing: Village Craftsmen

Photography: Raymond F. Errett and Nicholas L. Williams except
for 25 Beetle (N. el Fituri) and 37 Deep Sea 1889 (Kunstmuseum
Düsseldorf)

*Special thanks to the Musée de l'Ecole de Nancy
without whose cooperation this exhibition would not have
been possible.*

*This exhibition is supported in part by a grant from
the National Endowment for the Arts and an indemnity from
the Federal Council on the Arts and the Humanities.*

CONTENTS

*Catalog entry by Philippe Garner

FOREWORD

"GALLÉ." Among glass collectors, the very name evokes images of pastel vases decorated with flowers and leaves amidst swirling mists. Their forms are strong and simple; their decoration is usually acid-etched, and sometimes it is sharpened with an engraver's wheel. Uniform, predictable, they are recognized instantly, even before the signature is found. Such are the commercial works of Emile Gallé's factory, works that perhaps were never even touched or seen by Gallé himself. In fact, they continued to be made for nearly three decades *after* his death.

But what of the pieces that reveal Gallé's intense interest in nature, his use of symbolism to express his deepest feelings, his manipulation of glass as a material in ways previously unknown? These pieces are the subject of this exhibition. They were made in limited quantities, no more than five or six of each model at the most—and some are thought to be unique. Each was a labor—of love, of inspiration, of genius, of patience. As you will see and discover in the catalog that follows, Gallé believed passionately that glass vessels could and should be more than functional containers. His glass objects were symbols of his poetic fantasy. And they were often tributes to the great men of science and the arts, works which were recognized, praised, and awarded prizes at World's Exhibitions from 1878 to 1904.

Today, his creations are valued not only because they are among the most significant works *in any material* of his day, but because of their relevance to contemporary art. Glass artists and collectors of contemporary glass have only to examine the objects in this catalog to realize how extraordinarily talented Gallé's workmen were. The seemingly accidental blazes of color, the constellations of air bubbles, the shimmering flecks of metal foils, and the entrapped figures of insects which seem to be floating in a haze are evidence of the demanding techniques that he developed and used. They give his objects a richness that is unparalleled in the history of glass. Likewise, his ability to make form and decoration one is remarkable. His work deserves—demands—close scrutiny. Such is the aim of this catalog and the wonderful exhibition it accompanies.

*   *   *

Gallé: Dreams into Glass would not have been possible without the generosity and cooperation of those in Europe and America who lent their treasures and contributed freely of their time and knowledge:

Lenders:
The Chrysler Museum, Norfolk, Virginia; N. El Fituri, Geneva, Switzerland; Musée de l'Ecole de Nancy, Nancy, France; Musée des Arts Décoratifs, Paris, France; Musée Pasteur, Institut Pasteur, Paris, France; Philadelphia Museum of Art, Philadelphia, Pennsylvania; Joanna Walker, England; and several private collections.

The forty masterworks in the exhibition were chosen after many consultations with those who know and revere Gallé's work:

Dr. Sigrid Barten, Museum Bellerive, Zurich; Marc Bascou; Dr. Henry Blount; Jean-Claude Brugnot; Yvonne Brunhammer, Musée des Arts Décoratifs; Max Bill; Jean Pierre Camard; Robert Charleston; Françoise Thérèse Charpentier, Musée de l'Ecole de Nancy; Bernard Danenberg; Gilles Désaulniers; Madame Desverjne, Musée de Conservatoire National des Arts et Métiers, Paris; Alastair Duncan, Christie, Manson and Woods; Gertrud Fünke-Kaiser; Philippe Garner, Sotheby Parke Bernet; Bernd Hakenjos, Hetjens Museum, Düsseldorf; Katherine Hiesinger, Philadelphia Museum of Art; Malcolm Hillier; Helga Hilschenz, Kestner-Museum, Hannover; Edgar Kaufmann, Jr.; Dr. Brigitte Klesse, Kunstgewerbemuseum, Cologne; Felix Marcilhac; Nancy O. Merrill, Chrysler Museum; Lillian Nassau; Ferdinand Neess; Jean-Luc Olivié, Musée des Arts Décoratifs; Annick Perrot, Musée Pasteur; Helmut Ricke, Kunstmuseum, Düsseldorf; Dr. Axel von Saldern, Museum für Kunst und Gewerbe, Hamburg; Jørgen Schou-Christensen, Det Danske Kunstindustrimuseum; Philippe Thiebaut, Musée D'Orsay, Paris; and Robert Walker.

Particular thanks are due those who helped identify the sometimes esoteric motifs on Gallé's vases. Pasteur Coupe: Dr. Paul Parkman, United States Food and Drug Administration; plant identification: Dr. Karl Niklas, Cornell University; Paul Stankard; Virginia Wright, The Corning Museum of Glass; sea creatures: Dr. John Heiser, Shoals Marine Laboratory (Cornell University); geology: Candace Quinn, Corning Glass Works; insect identification: Carolyn Klass and E. Richard Hoebeke, (Cornell University).

The translations from Emile Gallé's *Ecrits pour l'Art* were done by Sima Godfrey, University of North Carolina, Chapel Hill; Catherine Mouly, and Monique Giausserand.

Special thanks are due the staff of The Corning Museum of Glass: Ray Errett and Nick Williams for photography, Priscilla Price, Joe Maio, Daryl Stratton, and Pat Driscoll for organization and installation of the exhibition; Phyllis Casterline and Donna Yeman for helping prepare the manuscript; Charleen Edwards for making welcome editorial suggestions and to Mary Lou Littrell whose catalog design speaks for itself.

Finally, and most importantly, to Thomas S. Buechner for his encouragement, creativity, and high standards. It was he who brought a painter's viewpoint to the photography and the objects in this catalog. It was he, as well, who designed the exhibition.

DWIGHT P. LANMON
Director

INTRODUCTION

EMILE GALLÉ, the man who turned many of his "dreams into glass," spent his creative life during an age of technological, scientific, and political explosion. Thomas Edison invented the electric light in 1879, Alexander Graham Bell spoke on his telephone in 1876, and Louis Pasteur developed a vaccine for rabies in 1885. Henry Ford built his first car in 1893, and Orville and Wilbur Wright made the first airplane flight in 1903, one year before Gallé's death. Gallé himself, born in 1846 into a family noted for its production of utilitarian ceramics and glass, subsequently contributed his own technical innovations to glassmaking.

Just two years after Gallé's birth, Europe was swept by revolutions: the workers and craftspeople of Paris overthrew Louis Philippe's monarchy in February of 1848. Reaction to the failure of these revolutions may have set the stage for the predominant style which Gallé was later to adopt and modify:

> "...the main source of the naturalistic outlook is the political experience of the generation of 1848: the failure of the revolution, the suppression of the June insurrection, and the seizure of power by Louis Napoleon. The

disappointment of the democrats and the general disillusionment caused by these events finds its perfect expression in the philosophy of the objective, realistic, strictly empirical natural sciences. After the failure of all ideals, of all utopias, the tendency is now to keep to the facts, to nothing but the facts."[1]

The artists considered naturalists included Emile Zola in literature, and Millet, Daumier, Courbet, and the Barbizon school of landscape painters. They, and Gallé, however, did not confine themselves to a slavish imitation of nature, to "nothing but the facts." Rather than refine his techniques to match precisely the colors and textures of the world around him, Gallé accepted and used the accidental and tried to add a *personal* element to his work. His naturalism turned impressionist and symbolist, following parallel trends in literature and painting of the 1880s and 1890s. By 1900 Gallé could speak of his "compatriots" and include Rodin, Puvis de Chavannes and Monet (*Ecrits*, p. 248), with whom he shared a common aesthetic.

Politically, Gallé's position is characterized by his support of Dreyfus. Alfred Dreyfus, a French officer of Jewish descent, was convicted (1894) of betraying military secrets and sent to Devil's Island. Evidence of Dreyfus's innocence was suppressed by the military. Emile Zola's stinging indictment (J'Accuse) became the cutting edge of a storm of controversy that split France into two camps. The case was a rallying point for those opposed to sacrificing the individual to the institution and to the conservative forces which had gained power since the Utopian revolutions of 1848. Yet the strong feelings were also patriotic in the sense that those defending Dreyfus believed he would never betray his country.

All of these events affected Gallé the patriot (see the Joan of Arc vase, 3) and lover of Justice. Gallé was deeply involved politically: he signed the petition of 1898 calling for a resolution of the Dreyfus case, even inscribed some vases urging action (one reads "All souls are ready/one of them, however, must take the first step/Why not be the one to begin?), and dedicated one important work to Joseph Reinach (Sea Horses, 34), who wrote the history of the case. Who knows what sea horses have to do with Dreyfus, but the peculiar textures of the piece may have been inspired by Reinach, about whom one of his enemies wrote "Reinach had a voice of wood and leather and used to leap from chair to chair, in pursuit of bare-bosomed lady guests, with the gallantry of a self-satisfied gorilla."[2]

The case is also significant because it "acted as a stimulus to the reexamination of the traditional ideologies on which both the defenders and the enemies of the accused captain had rested their case."[3] It represented a reaction against the naturalistic outlook, a return to ideals after hard "facts" had proven just as elusive as ideas (key evidence in the case proved to be forged). From this turbulent background of immense technological growth and social upheaval came impressionism and symbolism.

Impressionism responds to the rush of innovation, increased speeds and shortened distances brought about by technology. Its artists try to capture fleeting moments – steam puffing from a locomotive, the horizon just before sunset. They seek to portray, not the steam or sunset itself, but their own *impressions* of each of these events. Symbolism is a response to the irrational in human behavior, those often unconscious elements revealed in dreams or when we lose our self control. As one

Emile Gallé in his atelier.

contemporary critic wrote,"An artist like Gallé makes us think of a quintessential abstraction that attempts to materialize the impalpable and to turn the dream into glass."[4] In fact, the role of the unconscious was just beginning to be investigated – Freud's "Interpretation of Dreams" appeared in 1900.

Nearly all the works in this exhibition were produced during the last fifteen years of Gallé's life, 1889-1904. They may be seen as symbolist or impressionist or even as products of Art Nouveau or 1890s' "end-of-the-century decadence." While many of the most famous practitioners of these styles openly revolted against *both* technology and nature – remember Des Esseintes, the chief character in Huysmans' book "Against Nature" – it was Gallé's brilliance to utilize nature *and* technology. This led him to a healthy sort of symbolism and a simple ethical approach to life that stressed individual welfare in the midst of rampant industrialism. In the sections that follow, Gallé's own words suggest his approaches to technique, nature, impressionism, symbolism, and illuminate his concern for alleviating human suffering.

Gallé as Glassmaker

Gallé's involvement with glass was inherited. His father, Charles, founded a crystal and ceramic business in 1845 in Nancy, about 175 miles east of Paris, although the manufacturing of objects occurred at Raon-l'Etape, Meisenthal, and Saint-Clement, all within 100 miles of Nancy. The Franco-Prussian war and German annexation of Alsace-Lorraine (where Meisenthal was located), resulted in the loss of one of his factories, and he therefore opened a factory in Nancy in 1871.[5]

The young Gallé, born May 4, 1846, was given a traditional education at the Lycée Imperial in Nancy; his preferences were for literature and natural sciences. But he complains: "I must confess that as far as I am concerned, I in no way received an education which was suited to facilitate the beginnings of my career. No professional instruction was disseminated among artistic workers, unless it was to the recruits of the straight-edge and the sawhorse.... For the artistic workman, it was something like the swimming lesson given to a dog when it is thrown into the river. (*Ecrits*, pp. 237-238). Gallé's "swimming lessons" were postponed while he traveled and studied from 1862-1864 in Germany and England to pursue an interest in music and decorative arts. The trip ended in Paris where he became friends with the glassmaker Eugène Rousseau. By the time he was twenty-eight his father had retired, and Gallé was in charge of the business.

His responsibilities at work and at home steadily increased; in 1875 he married Henriette Grimm, and his first child, Thérèse, was born in 1877. From about 1889-1896,[6] probably because of increased demand for his products, Gallé had glassware produced for him at Burgun, Schwerer & Cie in Meisenthal.

The years 1889 to 1904 were the period of Gallé's maturity and success as a glassmaker. From 1900 there is a charming description of the workshops; at that time he employed some 300 people:

"In 1883, you built enormous studios for the production of faience, glassware and a new industry, cabinetmaking. It is in the context of this fine factory – open to the public through your own generous hospitality – that your works should best be viewed in order to appreciate fully the character and variety of your production.

The factory is surrounded by tall trees that evoke a sense of peace and calm; the tranquility of this suburban site is broken only by the occasional bugle call from the neighboring barracks. Once the visitor has crossed the threshold, however, he may look forward to more and more surprises and satisfactions. At the right time of year, in the middle of the courtyard, beds of decorative flowers delight the eye while they also provide a constant source of instruction for your personnel. In the main building, a model of genuine architectural elegance, the work is divided up methodically. In one room, the cabinetmakers select, assemble, cut out and apply the thin strips of precious wood that will adorn tables, consoles, jewelry cases, mirrors, and other furniture of all shapes that is kept in an adjoining studio. In another space, craftsmen prepare the models and painters decorate the faience-ware that will be fed into a series of muffles; from these bellies of fire they emerge in full resplendence. Elsewhere spindles and engraving wheels score and flute glass, enriching it with the most delicate engravings. In yet another room, specialists cast, chisel, and patina the bronze mounts that will complete pieces of furniture. In the middle, a room filled with drawings, plans, pieces of glass and wood, little phials and the entire arsenal of a chemist; this is your study, the scholarly retreat in which your ideas, inventions and desires are elaborated and from which they will disseminate. It is in this room that I see you just as Victor Prouvé painted you, holding in

Interior of Edouard Hannon's house in Brussels showing the Dragonfly Coupe (23) on the table beneath lamp with domed shade. The house was decorated with furnishings by Gallé and Louis C. Tiffany.

one hand a long-necked vase in warm transparent shades that you scrutinize anxiously, searching for the right decoration that will complete it. Farther on, in an enormous hall, a number of furnaces liquify the glass that powerful lungs or the pressure of molds will transform into vases, bowls, flagons, and the thousands of fantasies that have earned your crystal-work its well-deserved celebrity. A second building contains completed samples of all these modes of production. I do not wish to push this little tour too much farther, for I fear I might be overstepping the limits of discretion in speaking of your private home and of those vast rooms in which you have assembled a selection of your most remarkable creations. There too lies a happy garden filled with the rarest plants and perfumes, like a beautiful book which you pore over endlessly, drawing your inspiration from the very source of nature."[8]

The portrait by Prouvé, done in 1892, is illustrated on page 26. Victor Prouvé, Gallé's lifelong friend and designer, had begun collaborating with him at an early age. Of this portrait he wrote to his mother: "Here is Gallé at work — not without hi's! and ho's! and ha's! and screams! and arms flung up in the air, but I couldn't care less, I have him. There is enough here to do something good... a symphony in gray and with a taste of crystal, of those crystals whose hues are so delicious."[9] Prouvé helped design such vases as Orpheus and Eurydice (1) and Joan of Arc (3).

Atelier at Gallé factory in 1900. Charles Gallé in background.

Gallé's successes meant medals and critical acclaim resulting from his participation in a wide variety of exhibitions, including the 1889 Paris Universal Exposition (see objects 1, 2, 3, 5), the Paris Universal Exposition of 1900 (12, 18), the Exposition de l'Ecole de Nancy, in Paris in 1903 (17) the Chicago Exposition of 1893, and the Saint Louis Exposition of 1904 (see 24). Works by Gallé were added to prominent collections, including those of Roger Marx (art critic, editor of *Gazette des Beaux-Arts;* objects 14, 19, 21), Edouard Hannon (industrialist; for his house in Brussels, 23), and the Philadelphia Museum of Art (24); Gallé's objects were presented to the Russian royal family and Louis Pasteur (4), were ordered by writers such as Marcel Proust[10] or dedicated to such notables as Sarah Bernhardt. The famous Mushroom Lamp (30) was designed as part of a dining room with a forest theme for Gallé's patron and friend in Nancy, J. B. Eugène Corbin, publisher of *Art et Industrie.* Corbin's house, with its fabulous art nouveau collections, was bequeathed to Nancy and became the core of the Musée de l'Ecole de Nancy, which has lent several important pieces to this exhibition (6, 13, 32, 36, 39). An entré into French society which enhanced Gallé's reputation was effected by the same man who helped introduce Marcel Proust: the fantastic Count Robert de Montesquiou-Fezensac. Montesquiou dedicated poetry to Gallé, and wrote about his glass.[11]

The critical reaction which attended Gallé's success and continues today has been both positive and negative, ranging from Roger Marx's comment of 1911:

"The boldness of his life and character shine through his work"[12]

to the condemnation of Gerald Reitlinger in his 1970 "The Economics of Taste":

"...Emile Gallé of *Art Nouveau* fame, the begetter of tortured elongated shapes in the color and texture of old, decayed bathroom sponges."[13]

But what of Gallé the artist? How did he see the working process which enabled him to achieve these triumphs (and no doubt an occasional soggy sponge, too)? A most revealing personal statement appears in his exposition notice for 1889:

> My own work consists above all in the execution of personal dreams: to dress crystal in tender and terrible roles, to compose for it the thoughtful faces of pleasure or tragedy, to assemble all the elements and carefully prepare the effective production of my future projects, to order technique in the service of preconceived works of art, and to weigh the operational scale of chance with possibilities for success at the time of the decisive operation, once called the master-work. In other words, insofar as I am capable, from the start, I impose upon it qualities I should like it to have – the material and its colorations, the material and its measures – in order to incarnate my dream and my design.
>
> Needless to say, all of these calculations can be, and often are, disrupted by unforeseen causes; but the very hazards of a craft in which fire collaborates, violently and brutally, often serve me in the most fortuitous way. . . . Thus it is, Gentlemen, that I am not only responsible for the uses that can be made of crystal but also for the point of departure in this adventure. I have sought to make crystal yield forth all the tender or fierce expression it can summon when guided by a hand that delights in it. And it is I who have infused it, as it were, with the means for touching us: the worrisome blackness or the delicate morbidezza of soft rose petals. Emile Gallé (*Ecrits*, pp. 350-352).

So Gallé sees his role – as both dreamer and director.

Nonetheless, this dreamer always sensitively acknowledged the individuals who helped him accomplish his lifetime work, including Prouvé, the painter Louis Hestaux, and many others. The insensitivity of nineteenth-century industrialism was his greatest regret:

> This was one of the errors, one of the bitter penalties of the age of industrialism with its excessive division of labor, its organized management located in a poisoned and artificial atmosphere far from the domestic hearth, the family, and the natural environment. The century that is about to end did not have its own popular art, that is to say, no art applied to useful objects and executed spontaneously, joyously by the various artisans of each craft. Emile Gallé (*Ecrits*, p. 226).

*   *   *

At the beginning of the nineteenth century colour in glass was something new. From c. 1680 to 1825 transparent, colourless glass with engraved and cut decorations had been the main product of makers of fine glass in most parts of Europe. [14]

What follows is intended to outline for the non-technically oriented reader some of the processes employed by Gallé to achieve his dreams in glass. Those seeking detailed technical information are referred to the full exposition notices and patent applications.[15] The brief discussion below includes several techniques: enameling, engraving, patina, and marquetry, the latter two developed in the late 1890s by Gallé.

(Fig. 1) Vase, blown, overlay and applied decoration, cut. Eugène Rousseau, France, dated 1884.

Many of Gallé's techniques are refinements or adaptations. The roots of his experiments with color were undoubtedly in Bohemia, Murano, and France and included Georges Bontemps (1799-1884) at the Choisy-le-Roi factory. The technical perfection required to produce paperweights during the so-called "classic" period (1845-1855) must also have provided valuable knowledge about color.

More directly, the work of the glassmaker Eugène Rousseau (1827-1891) was significant. His revival of cased glass, imitations of gemstones, and assimilation of motifs drawn from Japanese art (Perry made his voyage to Japan in 1853, and there was a display of Japanese art at the 1867 World's Fair in Paris) all influenced Gallé's early work. A vase in The Corning Museum of Glass collection (Fig. 1) exemplifies all these influences: it is cased, imitative of carnelian, and assymetrical as in Japanese art. Orpheus and Eurydice (1), with its striations of color from metal oxides, also indicates Rousseau's influence; such oxides could never be completely controlled (engraving, for example, could be controlled to a much greater degree), and both Gallé and Rousseau learned how to use these accidental effects advantageously. In the case of Orpheus the red torrent of oxides becomes "a flaming meteor."

Among Gallé's earliest interests was enameling on glass, which he seems to have begun about 1873.[16] Many of the enamels were inspired by historical themes drawn from ancient Egypt, Islam, Japan, etc. The technical investigations of Philippe-Joseph Brocard (d. 1896) were also important. Because we focus on the later work of Gallé, none of these early enamels is included in the exhibition; nevertheless, two pieces of later dates serve to illustrate the technique (5, 6).

*   *   *

In his book *Le Verre et le Cristal* (Glass and Crystal), Mr. Jules Henrivaux, director of Saint-Gobain, says, 'Mr. Gallé has sought to bring back into favor for a very special, and, it must be said, very restricted audience, an art which shone with some brilliance in antiquity, as well as in the Sixteenth and Seventeenth centuries, that of glass engraving, by making it yield its all and associating it with enamels on the same piece, in spite of great dangers and frequent losses. In recent years, color had completely eclipsed the charming art of etching in the public eye.' (*Ecrits*, p. 311).

By the 1880s color in glass was so dominant that engraving would appear, as above, in need of revival! The enameled *Magnolia* vase (5) is a good example of the unusual combination with engraving that Henrivaux describes.

Gallé had definite feelings, however, about how contemporary engraving should function:

How I Have Interpreted Crystal Engraving
You are no doubt familiar, Gentlemen, with skillful examples of engraving where the crystal, beautiful as it may be in itself, is overwhelmed, as it were, beneath the weight of such long, meticulous handiwork – work that seems unconscious of time, of the object and of life itself. It is almost as if one had forgotten to turn off a magical machine that robot-like engravers use to create the lasting, impeccable and imperturbable sculpture of cold master-pieces. 'Admirable workers,' exclaims M. Bonnaffé, 'as remarkable to be sure as the galley-slave who carves a fully rigged ship out of a coconut with the tip of his pocketknife.' 'Cold, hard objects,' responds in turn M. Eugène Guillaume, with reference to certain engravings on precious stones, 'like those produced by Jeuffroy at the turn of this century. They express only the boredom of the artist and the difficulties that the practice of his profession set in his way.'

In keeping with the noble lessons of these masters of French art, I have found in engraving above all a means of expression, a means to bring forth out of warm and living material all the elements that have been consolidated within it. Even in those pieces that took longest to elaborate, I never forgot the need for moderation: the enthusiasms of the artist must not suffocate the material from which he composes his work.

I would hope therefore that you might discover in the materials that I set before you and in the execution of the hand, all the *flaws* – this sooner than silence, than dryness of execution, than mere love of prettiness, than the monotony of technique or the impression of boredom! In order to avoid the appearance of mechanical work, we have therefore been more casual in the description of accessory detail: we have concentrated all our attention on one given point. In the presentation of a harvest of fine, ripened fruit, one sees the side of the sun just out of focus. We have sought to avoid the appearance of stamped impressions, of molds and of reproductions; we have let the contours of our engravings flow into the background. Our tools have marked their form in crystal, and with that form marked too all the tenderness and respect of the craftsman for his material.

If one were to make plaster molds of my engraved works, stripped of their color and soft relief, there would remain, no doubt, very little to speak of; nevertheless, it would be clear that these were crystals and not bronzes or ivories. Emile Gallé (*Ecrits*, pp. 347-348).

This approach to engraving is evident throughout the exhibition; as in the head of Orpheus (1), or the fins of the Sea Horses (34). In some cases, Gallé also used acid etching to rough out a form, for example in Joan of Arc (3). "Acid reaches easily into those areas that the spindle cannot touch." (*Ecrits*, p. 347).

Notice Gallé's remarks about allowing the tools to leave their mark, and so convey the artisan's tenderness and respect for the material. As we have seen, one of Gallé's critiques of industrialism was that it displaced the workman's joy in his own work – something which Gallé is obviously trying to restore in his new approach to engraving. With the development of patina and marquetry he underscores his convictions.

*   *   *

One way to encourage a sense of freedom in the worker, a joy in working, and understanding of the whole object, is to provide an opportunity for spontaneous decisions. The marquetry and patina processes offered such opportunities. Partly inspired by ancient glassmakers who applied threads and other types of decoration to the hot mass of glass and by paperweight makers who arranged numerous glass canes to form floral bouquets and then trapped them forever within a sphere of colorless crystal, marquetry involved the addition of bits, fragments, thin laminations, or other kinds of glass onto the hot glass body of a vessel. Patina utilized ashes from wood or coal and other specially prepared particles to produce textures on or under the vessel surfaces. Both approaches were often combined with engraving, acid etching, etc., for maximum effect. Thistles (12) is a good example of marquetry, while the surfaces on Sea Horses (34), Rhubarb (17), and Sea Lily (33) are patinated. The Dragonfly (24) and Pines (21, 22) combine both processes with engraving.

The successful development by Gallé of these various approaches to glassmaking restored self respect to the workman and has been beautifully summed up in relation to marquetry by Jules Henrivaux (director of Saint Gobain):

To be sure, the technique demands great skill. It is hardly a simple task to insert and place one hundred or more pieces of glass mosaic on a vase – no more simple than the successive reheatings that must be done each time or the regular process of stripping and fashioning that is called in the specialized language of engraving *ciselure* [sculpture], a process quite distinct from that of cameo. Nevertheless, it must be said that the craftsman,

View of the Gallé glasshouse and employees.

charged with doing this inlay, derives great pleasure as he goes along from the delightful effects produced by the assemblage of glass pieces that he transposes one at a time. At that moment, he becomes a decorative artist, a landscape artist and a colorist; as he carefully works his stained glass into the mass, he produces, like the painter, a thoughtful work of feeling and taste. He himself sees and understands the significance of everything that emerges from his efforts. He brings something of his own imagination to the work of his fingers and then stands back to judge the charm that is born of that fruitful collaboration. In short, he develops his faculties of attention and discernment out of an obligation to his own very special talents. [17]

It is this working process which *encourages* spontaneity and freedom in the workman. This seems especially true in objects such as the small Pines (22) where the exceptional detail could have only been achieved by an artist/workman working with understanding and inspiration.

We should remind ourselves, however, that it was Gallé's ideal to turn craftsmen into artists. One wonders to what extent he *was* able to transform his workmen with this system and to what extent he already employed artists who were simply best suited to work this way.

Gallé: Naturalist, Impressionist, Symbolist
In her introduction to Gallé's collected writings, his widow Henriette Gallé-Grimm

asserts that

"...if Emile Gallé has renewed the decorative arts, it is because he has studied plants, trees, flowers, both as an artist and a scholar." (*Ecrits*, p. VI).

When confronted with issues of design, Gallé often asked himself "how nature had resolved the problem." (*Ecrits*, pp. 267-268). Here, his education served him well:

"Luckily—and here, I must once again speak of myself—the love of the flower reigned in my family: it was hereditary passion. It was salvation. I knew something of the natural sciences. I had followed the botanizatons of Godron, the author of the *Flores de Lorraine et de France*. On his crystals, his porcelains, my father had made studies of fields and meadows, reproductions of Graminacea and blooming grasses." (*Ecrits*, p. 239).

The extent to which Gallé depended on nature for his decorative themes is revealed in this catalog—there is no single object that does not draw on nature. Nearly every piece includes plant life, and only Orpheus and Eurydice (1), Joan of Arc (3) and Geology (13) confine themselves to classical or inorganic subject matter. But no pieces are slavish imitations. Instead, nature served Gallé as a launch pad, allowing him to break away from tradition and reach new heights:

"The jury will please note that Gallé always takes nature as his point of departure, and that he takes pains to free himself from it in time to attain a personal character and accent." (*Ecrits*, p. 317).

In discussing furniture design, he rejected Greek classicism and welcomed nature (*Ecrits*, pp. 256-7). Even the influence of Japanese art is significant because of its focus on nature (Edmond de Goncourt—Gallé's friend—writer, a leader of the Naturalism movement, collector, was among the first to introduce Japanese art in France): "Amid so many reasons for which to honor this benefactor [Goncourt] of spontaneous art, there is one which the school of modern crafts must loudly proclaim: in his writings he declared that 'ancient Japan is desperately monotonous.' That all the enchanting decoration in Japanese art which is worthy of appreciation by people of taste is *modern, yes, modern, of the nineteenth century,* that the most pliant bronzes are those of artists dead twenty, thirty, or forty years ago.', that this 'marvelous, unique, incomparable art' must be attributed to the revolution introduced into design by the liberation of classical styles and by a return to direct, loving observation, to the very collaboration of nature." (*Ecrits*, p. 178).

Again in the essay on contemporary furniture design, we get a rare glimpse into how he translated nature's gifts into decorative motifs, in this case, moldings:

Take directly the peduncula either of the leaf or of the flower of certain of the Orchidea, the Umbellifera of our woods. Study the striations which furrow them. They are alternatively thick and thin. Examine them under strong magnification. They have the look of veritable cabinetmaker's, architect's moldings, with lights opposed to darknesses, roundnesses to planes. You will find there moldings other than the *bec-de-corbin,* and *cymaises* from the Greeks which are not repeated. Moreover, this structure sometimes moves from bottom to top, from left to right, in reverse direction. Here and there it is interrupted at regular intervals, masterfully, by the insertion of leaves and branches. To learn the secret of these combinations, take cuttings, multiply the sketches, but compare them to the living model. You will be surprised to find these anatomies increasingly full of charms and secrets, always superior in beauty to the adaptations based on it. You will be surprised that man has so little delved into this infinite repertory to replenish his arts of furniture. (*Ecrits*, pp. 262-263)

Still, Gallé's naturalism was never very close to the precision of writers like Goncourt or Zola. Rather, he thought of nature as full of messages to be deciphered: "Baudelaire has expressed for us most grandly this concept of the harmonies that resonate throughout the immensity of creation.

> *The pillars of Nature's temple are alive*
> *And sometimes yield perplexing messages;*
> *Forests of symbols between us and the shrine*
> *Remark our passage with accustomed eyes."*

(Trans. Richard Howard, *Les Fleurs du Mal*, Boston:Godine, 1982) (From *Ecrits*, p. 220)

*   *   *

Gallé worked in many styles, from revivals of ancient Egypt, medieval Islam, classical Greece and Rome (Orpheus and Eurydice, 1) to naturalism. Two styles, symbolism and impressionism, were especially relevant for their effect on his later work.

In a sense, impressionism is a refined naturalism as defined by the writer Emile Zola, who noted that impressionists study "...the changing aspects of nature according to the countless conditions of hour and weather....They pursue the analysis of nature all the way to the decomposition of light, to the study of moving air, of color nuances, of incidental transitions of light and shadow, of all the optical phenomena which make a horizon appear variable and so difficult to represent."[18] This theory is supported by many of Gallé's own remarks, for example: "Thus in nature the most disparate colorings melt under the magic spells of the atmosphere." (*Ecrits*, p. 209).

Look at Autumn (7), where the leaves change so dramatically as the light changes. Or the Hazel Tree (11), receptacle for a premature, tentative decoration almost washed away by winter rains. Pieces like Orchids (19, 20) and Tadpoles (32) reflect the changing seasons, while in Blue Melancholy (38) the flowers seem covered in spots by a misty haze. The marquetry process itself parallels experiments by some post-impressionists. The "cut out," flattened figures in Seurat's *La Grande Jatte* might be compared to the thin glass inlays used by Gallé.

It was natural for artists to move from impressionism to symbolism. Instead of recording nature, many artists recorded their own ideas. "Symbols are the points at which ideas become concrete," Gallé wrote. (*Ecrits*, p. 218). A few of his early works are allegorical. Allegory in symbolism parallels the historical revival of antique styles in the decorative arts. In Orpheus and Eurydice (1) a popular classical theme is translated into decoration for a vase, and our interpretation of its meaning is determined by the Orpheus legend.

But many symbolists came to feel that allegory lacked potency for at least two reasons. First, the themes from which allegories were derived were often esoteric, forgotten, outmoded – much as imitation mosque lamps could never hope to serve the functional purpose of their prototypes and so became dust-gathering curiosities. Second, allegory was too precise; it didn't allow the viewer to exercise enough imagination and so evoke the sense of mystery symbolists sought. New symbols, in tune with the 1890s, had to be found.

Gallé found his symbols in nature: "Indeed, love of nature must always lead to symbolism: the popular flower loved by all will always occupy a principal role in ornamental symbolism." (*Ecrits*, p. 218).

For example, the thistle (12) could represent defiance; Olives and Pines, peace (10); Grapes (15) the transforming qualities of wine.

It may be that the most powerful symbols, those most like dreams, are the least allegorical, evoke the greatest mystery, and make us guess at their meaning. In Gallé's work, pieces dealing with sea themes (Deep Sea, 36, or the Hand, 39) illustrate this most forcefully:

> *Man – a free man – always loves the sea*
> *And in its endlessly unrolling surge*
> *Will contemplate his soul as in a glass*
>
> . . .
>
> *– who has sounded to its depths the human heart?*
> *And who has plucked its riches from the sea? –*
> *So jealously they guard their secrets both!*

(Baudelaire; Trans. Richard Howard)

These secrets of the Ocean are brought forth to us by brave deep-sea divers. They empty their marine harvest which passes from the laboratory to the studios of decorative art and to the museums of models. They draw and publish these undreamt-of materials for the artist: enamels and cameos from the sea. And soon, crystalline jelly-fish will inspire new shadings and original curves in chalices of glass. Emile Gallé (*Ecrits*, pp. 224-225).

*   *   *

From the turn of the century, Gallé's workshops produced objects of astonishing virtuosity, each fraught with symbolic mystery. One wonders . . . could he have had an intimation that only four years remained to see that his dreams were realized? We recall that while still vigorous he had written: "Coldness indeed! Is it not the business of snow to be white, of the glacier to be blue? Anemia! Not everyone can be anemic. I happen to like anemia. If everything were all strength and force, we would have to bid adieu to grace, adieu to harmony." (*Ecrits*, pp. 115-116).

Gallé died on September 23, 1904, from an illness diagnosed as leukemia.[19] At

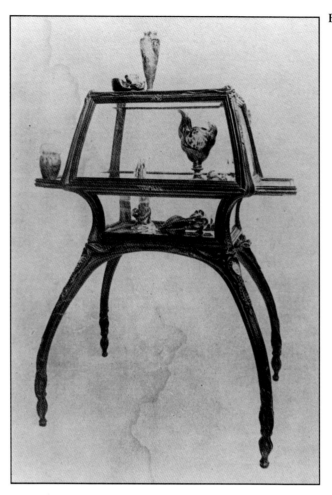

fifty-eight, he was the premier glass artist of his generation, deeply involved in the pursuit of innovative techniques to turn dreams about nature into glass.

His disillusion at the failure of industrialization to meet the needs of individual workers and his involvement with the Dreyfus affair, where a single individual had been so unjustly persecuted, reinforced his philosophy that suffering is inevitable, but through suffering we may reach a state of grace and harmony. He therefore saw his work as part of a healing process to share with mankind the beauty scattered throughout the world: "The path is rocky. And I am weak. What do I care for the painter? Give me the decorative artist: he is the good Samaritan that I long for. From the glassmaker I ask for perfumes in his vases . . . ." (*Ecrits*, p. 199).

Today we revere and appreciate Gallé's work for its revealing interpretations of nature's mystery. The photographs and catalog which follow portray a man of his time who probed beyond his time and one who both drew from glass and imposed his philosophy upon it. Gallé makes us look at his vases not only as fantastic works of art but as purveyors of his own heightened sense of the symbolism of nature and the value of human endeavor.

WILLIAM WARMUS
Associate Curator, Twentieth-Century Glass

Emile Gallé, portrait by Victor Prouvé, 1892. Collection of the Musée de l'Ecole de Nancy (photo courtesy Philippe Garner).

CATALOG

Note: Numbers 1, 2, 3, 4, 11, and 40 are English translations of Gallé's original titles. Other objects have been given titles to reflect the themes they represent. Only exhibitions held during Gallé's lifetime are listed.

1a) Orpheus and Eurydice

1b) Head of Orpheus

1) ORPHEUS AND EURYDICE

1c) Reverse side

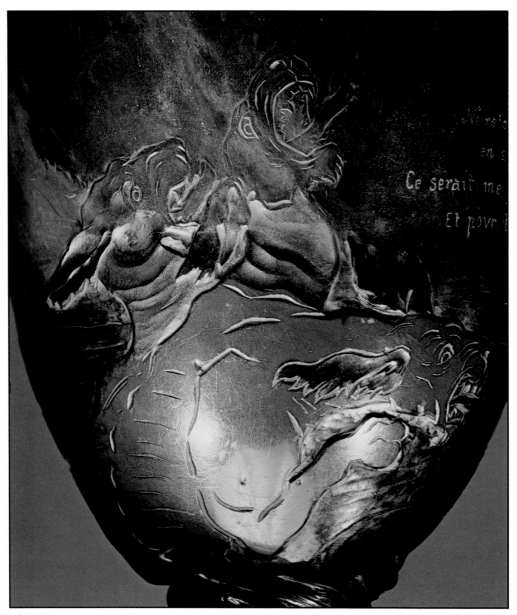

1d) Cerberus

It has caught my fancy to work with awesome onyxes and to wrap a vase in streams of lava and pitch; to enlist the Styx and the Acheron Rivers on the foot of a bowl, to use a flaming meteor and the gases of hell to separate Orpheus from Eurydice who lies faint in a sooty brown crystal.

Emile Gallé (*Ecrits*, p. 351).

ORPHEUS, renowned in ancient Greek mythology as a poet and musician, is shown here in the Underworld. He had gone there to persuade its lord, Hades, to release his wife Eurydice, who had died from the bite of a viper. Charmed by Orpheus' playing on the lyre (visible below Orpheus) Hades agreed to release Eurydice on condition that Orpheus lead her out without looking back until she reached the sunlight. All was lost when he looked back prematurely. Orpheus is shown reaching out for Eurydice as Cerberus, the three-headed guard dog of the Underworld, barks (just visible below and to the left of Eurydice, 1a).

The inscriptions read:

> Turn back no more;
> That would be to lose me twice
> And for all time...

– and –

> What, oh, what utter madness hath ruined, she cried to him then,
> Both me the all-hapless and thee, O Orpheus? Back am I called By
> the ruthless Fates, and with slumber my swimming eyes are palled.
>> Virgil, Georgics, IV, 11. 494-496; trans. Arthur S. Way,
>> The Georgics of Virgil, London: Macmillan, 1912

Much of Gallé's work from the 1870s and eighties shows the influence of historical or classical themes, or of his immediate predecessors such as Eugène Rousseau (1827-1891) who made vases with encased oxides (like the "red torrent" in Orpheus 1a), often based on Oriental forms. The form of Orpheus, which appears to be classical and symmetrical, on close examination is seen to be lopsided (1a). In other words, rather than trying to imitate a classical, man-made shape which does not appear in nature, the twisted, deep amber-red base marks the beginning of a metamorphosis toward more organic-looking structures such as Rhubarb (17). Gallé seems to ask: how can I use what is inherent in glassmaking – oxides for color, the inevitable bubbles, etc. – to represent fire, night, water? Gallé makes us simultaneously aware of details for what they are (e.g., red oxides in the glass) and what they represent (e.g., fire), and opens the way for the exploitation of accidental effects which can become decorative motifs.

Parallel with this, Gallé encouraged his engravers in a spontaneous use of their tools. In an age of exquisite, but frequently restrained and painstaking craftsmanship (Northwood, etc.), this work has a liveliness of particular strength; notice, for example, the head and hair of Orpheus (1b). The fact that the hand of the maker is so evident in every wheel cut is analogous to the vigorous brush work of Millet, L'Hermite – even Van Gogh – rather than Bougereau, LeFevbre, or Jerome, who tended to subordinate signs of spontaneity in favor of the much admired high finish of the period.

By selectively casing colorless glass with deep amber-red and cutting through this dark layer, the artist develops something akin to an "ethics of light": while wicked Cerberus glints in the darkness of the base, existing solely in cool reflected light, good Orpheus and Eurydice glow in a transmitted light.

1e) **Base**

Dated 1888-1889 · H. 26.5 cm, D. 17 cm
Blown, internal inclusions of dark red and brownish-black; cased; cut, engraved, gilt.
Signed: (Base) *Vitrarius faciebat Emile Gallé/Lotharing^s Nanceiis [sic] E (Cross of Lorraine) G 1888-1889/Effigies inv. amicus V-Prouvé/Nanc. (?)/egregius pictor,* (friend, inventor of images, and fine painter, V. Prouvé, Nancy.) with blowpipe and engraving lathe in the background, and "V" formed as a conical, footed drinking glass.
Inscribed (on band around shoulder): *Qvis et me inqvit, miseram, et te perdidit Orphev Qvis tantvs fvror? En itervm crvdelia retro Fata vocant, condit qve natantia lvmina Somnvs. Virg;* (to left of Eurydice): *Ne retournez plus /En arrière/Ce serait me perdre deux fois/et pour toujours AE (crown).*
Collection: Musée des Arts Décoratifs, Paris, Inventory No. 11975
Exhibited at the 1889 Paris Universal Exposition

2a)   Cupid Chasing Black Butterflies

2b) Detail showing butterflies

2) CUPID CHASING BLACK BUTTERFLIES

IN THE MIDST of a deadly twilight, a fussily engraved cupid confronts, with an immense harpoon-like arrow, the back of a butterfly so large, so black, so forbidding that it and its companions appear the heralds of death or horror rather than blossom-like insects. The paradox of coupling the benign and the brutal – like beauty and the beast – gives new meaning to the oversentimentalized subject matter of the period.

Above the bulbous body of the vessel is a cylindrical collar inscribed *Cupid Chasing Black Butterflies*. The domed cover, surmounted by a colorless finial, is decorated with a motif including crossed arrows; the knop of the stem is also colorless, but the other surfaces are of a black glass about which Gallé writes:

> BLACK *(hyalith)*
> This composition could appear rather sad; but etching brings to light clouded greenish hues that the engraver can manipulate successfully...a small vase has been very finely etched with a *Cupid Chasing Black Butterflies*. I think I can attribute the gray glint that renders this material so iridescent to the contact during production with the carbon deposits of the glory hole that provoke an incipient reduction of the iron peroxide. (*Ecrits*, p. 337).

Some of the fine engraving enriches the surface at an almost subliminal level: small diamond-point scratches create furry edges around the butterflies and make stars from the tiny craters formed by broken surface bubbles.

Dated 1889 · H. 15 cm, D. (rim) 6.2 cm · Blown; cased; cut, engraved. Two parts.
Signature: (Base) *Emile Gallé fecit Nancy/Exposition 1889. Paris* around butterfly wings
Inscription (below rim): *L'amour chasse les papillons noirs*
Collection: Musée des Arts Décoratifs, Paris, France, Inventory No. 27983
Exhibited at the 1889 Paris Universal Exposition

3a)   Joan of Arc

3) JOAN OF ARC

The peace we need is that they go back home.

(inscription on the vase)

THE FRANCO-PRUSSIAN WAR (1870-1871) cut Gallé off from his factory operations at Meisenthal; Nancy itself was occupied in 1870, and part of Lorraine (the region around Nancy) was annexed to Germany. Gallé always seems to have been devoted to the concept of a great *national popular art* (*Ecrits*, p. 228), and his experiences as an army volunteer during the war surely increased his patriotism. Thus, it is not uncommon for Gallé to employ nationalistic themes in his work such as the Cross of Lorraine (frequently added near his signature). Among patriotic emblems, Joan of Arc would be a natural choice: France's greatest heroine, she was born near the region of Lorraine and visited Nancy. She becomes a pure symbol for that "national decor" which is:

...Celtic, Gallic, proud child of a harsh nature, child of the Druids and of the bards, returning always – after all the invasions, those from the South and those from the East, after all the intermixtures and all the fashions, Roman or Barbarian – to its nature, to nature, to its free spirit, to the source, to the native flora and fauna, to the sheer joy of the craftsman freely decorating his work in his home, to his taste, and with love. (Emile Gallé, *Ecrits*, p. 220)

The central medallion depicts Joan of Arc in left profile, holding a sword in her right hand; behind her we see the heads of her soldiers, while riding ahead of her (on the medallion's right side) is a soldier holding a lance, astride a horse whose head alone is visible. The devices below the rim are "spearhead" ornaments. One side of the vase is decorated with the inscription (quoted at the beginning of this entry) within a circle with two arms that spiral outward; the base of the glass piece fits down into the removable metal base.

Gallé's description of the vase in his notices for the 1889 Paris Universal Exposition shows his interest in the juxtaposition of different techniques:

> For the engraving of my work, I have made use of all the resources available: patinas, both lustrous and mat, soft textures that are pleasing to the eye and the touch, bas-reliefs, cameos, foregrounds embossed in the round and backgrounds with a stained-glass effect, with lithophanic* reliefs that are carved with spindles of the finest dimension. You will find such an example in the work on the large vase, (No. 68) *(Joan of Arc)*. Here the opaque cameo** engraving of the foreground surface moves into stained-glass work in the deeper surfaces, in such a way that the work remains of interest both in its refraction and reflection of light. (*Ecrits*, p. 346)

Figures in the central medallion (3b and 3c) reveal an interesting aspect of Gallé's handling of cool and warm light. The light that reflects from dark surfaces is cool, while the light transmitted through the amber glass is warm. Joan of Arc and her soldiers depend upon transmitted amber light, while the foreground knight with lance depends upon blue-gray reflected light (b). The result is a dramatic division of space (notice how it disappears in c), concurrent with ideas in contemporary illustration wherein the viewer is pulled into the scene by the seeming nearness of part of the subject matter – the looming foreground figure in this case. While Gallé's juxtaposition of two types of engraving in the medallion achieves an original effect (the division of space), the chipped obsidian-like implements in the upper frieze (resulting from acid-etching) seem to stand in isolation. They contrast sharply with the detailed medallion, but neither affects the other. It is as if two separate creative forces were at work. And although a sense of exploited accident is evident in much of Gallé's work, the elongated bubbles which run through the figure of Joan and across the mane of her horse are not utilized. At the same time, the spontaneous engraving of Joan's head is reminiscent of the forcefulness of the Orpheus head (1b).

Dated 1889 · H. 43.1 cm; D. (max) 22 cm; D. (rim) 15.5 cm
Blown; cased; acid-etched, cut, engraved. Metal base.
Signature (base): *Nanceus Faciebat/Emile Gallé/1889* and *amicus V. Prouvé Lotharing: Puellam del mea: pictoregr.*
Inscription (in circle on one side):
La/Paix qu il/faut c'est/qu'ils s'en/retourent/chex eux
Collection: Private
Exhibited at the 1889 Paris Universal Exposition

*Note: Lithophane is porcelain impressed with figures that are made distinct by transmitted light; the glass decorating technique of lithophane has its prototypes in Bohemia and France from the 1840s on.

**Gallé seems to refer here to the engraved medallion. His use of the term differs from recent definitions, as, for example, in *Cameo Glass, Masterpieces from 2000 Years of Glassmaking*, Corning, New York: The Corning Museum of Glass, 1982, p. 130: "CAMEO GLASS: Glass of one color cased or covered with one or more layers of contrasting color. These outer layers are carved in relief by various techniques to produce a design which stands out from the background." *Opaque* engraving probably refers to the area around the horse and soldier on the right in the medallion.

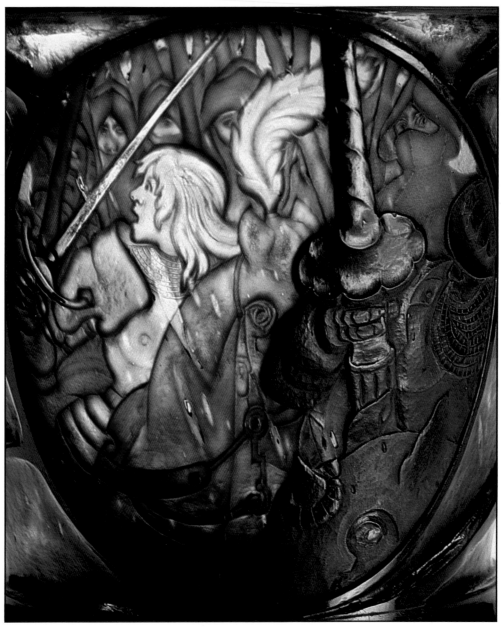

3b) Medallion in transmitted and reflected light

3c) Medallion in reflected light

4a) Pasteur Coupe

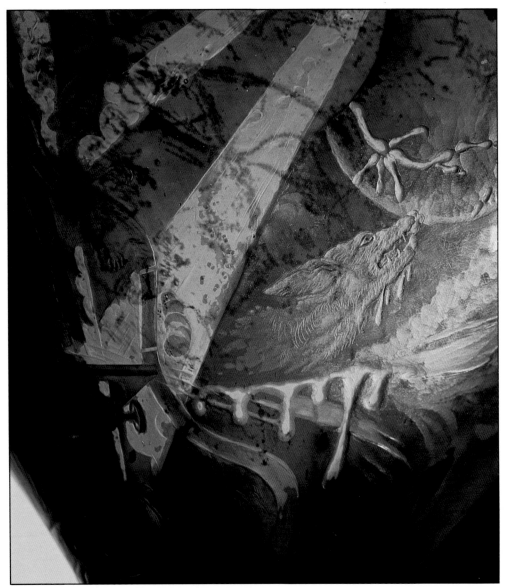

4b) Detail showing rabid dog to right of microscope

4) PASTEUR COUPE

I move about in meditation,
And at all moments a certain instinct obliges me
To seek and find what lies behind the suffering of men.
                                                    Victor Hugo

(inscription on the coupe)

THE DECORATION IS COMPLEX and at times so jumbled that it is difficult to interpret. On one side (4a) is a coiled python (left), a microscope (center), pterodactyl-like winged creature (immediately right of the microscope), white cones of light (two directed from the upper right edge of the vase toward the microscope; one from the mirror at the base of the microscope straight up), and a dog with rabies (right center below the cones of light and disks). On another side (4c), thorns rise from the base, and a plant pushes its branch above (coming from upper right).

The coupe (ceremonial bowl or goblet) was presented to Louis Pasteur by the Ecole-Normale Superiéure to mark his seventieth birthday. Gallé's decorations relate to some of Pasteur's great discoveries; these, along with the creative process behind the piece were discussed in a manuscript by Gallé (4d and *Ecrits* pp. 148-154, reprinted at the end of this entry).

Gallé calls the coupe an "innoculated" glass. Within the brown amber soup of the cone form, elements appear to float over and under each other, some flat (the microscope), others in the round (the dog), edges rigid or amorphous. Again, as in Cupid Chasing Black Butterflies (2), we see the tendency to outline by engraving, forming contrasting two- and three-dimensional edges.

Gallé's putting together of unrelated elements is especially evident here: the microscope looks like a drawing from a medical equipment catalog; the dog is of the Gustav Doré variety of realism while the views of microbes look like the plates in a biology textbook. Does all this activity perhaps anticipate the aesthetic of early Hollywood with its spotlight beams and photo montages?

Another Gallé characteristic is the use of opposing sides of a piece to develop narratives. In many botanical vases, the life cycle of a plant is depicted (for example, see the Orchids, 19 and 20). In the Pasteur Coupe, the sources of pestilence appear on one side; on the other side "effective relief": the balm of pity and the verses of Hugo. Pasteur's successful pursuit of remedies to human suffering must have been an inspiration to Gallé who, in 1900, wrote that the work of art "...must be a struggle for the justice in us and the justice around us. And life in the 20th century shall thus never lack for joy, art, or beauty." (*Ecrits*, p. 228).

4c) Reverse side

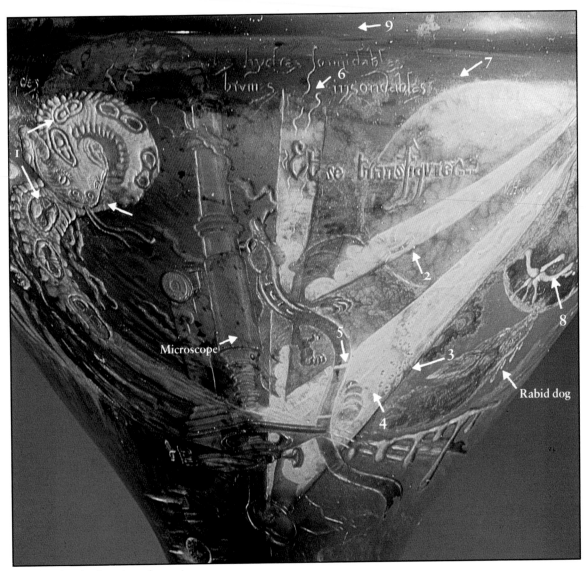

Detail indicating location of organisms, page 47

The organisms which decorate the vessel are in most cases clearly recognizable, and include:

1) streptococcus pneumoniae	The figure "8"shapes on the python (4a). Pasteur was the first to isolate this organism (19th-century name: Diplococcus pneumoniae Weichselbaum)
2)anthrax bacillus	Illuminated in the uppermost cone of light below the word "Transfigurer" (4a). Pasteur showed that the weakened bacteria could be used to vaccinate sheep and cows (19th-century name: Bacille de charbon).
3) streptococcus pneumoniae	Illuminated in the lower cone of light, just above the neck of the rabid dog (4b); same as the python decoration but in lower magnification.
4) adult silkworm	Below the streptococcus and to the left of the dog–a series of overlapping circles (4b). Pasteur's studies of the diseases of silkworms stimulated his interests in infectious disease problems.
5) clostridium septicum	The pterodactyl form to the right of the microscope (4a) is a diagrammatic representation of one member of a group causing gas gangrene, discovered by Pasteur in 1877 (19th-century name: Vibrion septique). The identification would be very tenuous without Gallé's stated intent in the essay that follows.
6) spirilla of stagnant water	One spirilla forms the "f" of "formidables," inscribed below the rim. (4a)
7) agar cultures in petri dishes	Circular forms in the upper right, crossed by the cones of light (4a); with whitish colonies on their surfaces.
8) yeast	The whitish shapes, cut into the lower petrie dish (just above the nose of the rabid dog in illustration 4b), are possibly yeast. Pasteur's research included these organisms, used in the brewing of beer and wine.
9) violet bacillus	Mentioned by Gallé in his essay, this may have inspired the overall violet tonality of the coupe (called chromobacterium violaceum today).

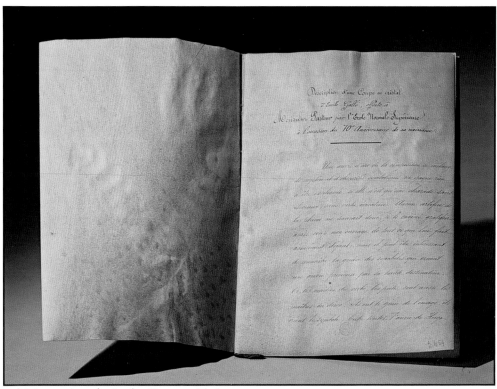

4d) Manuscript submitted to Pasteur with the coupe

Dated 1892 · H. 24.9 cm, D. (max.) 22.3 cm

Blown; inclusions; cased; engraved, probably acid etched; on metal base (which has incised microbe-like motifs).

Signed (on base): *à Monsieur/Pasteur/L'Ecole Normale Superieure/1892;* (lower right on thorn side): *Emile Gallé*

Inscribed: (below rim on microscope side):

> *On verra le troupeau des Hydres formidables*
> *Sortir, monter du fond des brumes insondables*
> *Et se transfigurer.*

(Upper left of side with thorns):

> *Toluifera Balsamum*

(On thorn side, right center)

> *Je vais*
> *Méditant, et toujours un instinct me ramène*
> *A connaître le fond de la souffrance humaine*

Collection: Musée Pasteur, Institut Pasteur, Paris

THE PASTEUR COUPE*

(Crystal goblet, presented to Pasteur by the Ecole Normale Supérieure on the occasion of his seventieth birthday, April 30, 1893)

A work of art in which mysterious and obscure symbols are blended into the composition has nothing to gain from explication, if it is itself nothing more than a hollow show with no eloquence or evocative virtue of its own. And so, no artful exercise of the pen can, I fear, redeem my little work after the fact for whatever faults it must have. It may remain nonetheless of interest to learn the origin of those symbols that decorate a work so precious by virtue of its esteemed destination. As it happens, the masters of language—Poets—are also masters of decoration. They have a genius for images; they create symbols. And the work of Victor Hugo is especially fertile for the artist. His texts are almost equal to the Scriptures in the abundant color of their visions, their lapidary language, and its applications that measure up to the highest statures. The poet exalts in painting for us men who desire, men who sacrifice, wise men, lovers of austere, sensual beauty, those who wander

...acquiring along the way
The benediction of the entire human race,

those who devote themselves to the search for truth and glide along lost in thought, hunched over questions of life and

the enigma in which being dissolves.

In my early attempts to come to terms with these images, these incantations first suggested to me a misty precipitate, the gray negation of all shades of color, the grouping of imprecise forms and livid opacities:

...the deep-eyed enigma that
stares at us relentlessly.

And then, sooty phantoms began to break through my conception of the decoration, symbols of empiricism, of the ignorance of causalities, monstrous forms of chimerical doctrines, miasmata and blastemata, *vague expressions,* in your own words, Master, *that respond to nothing tangible.*

Suddenly all sorts of shady notations took form on my paper, bizarre adaptations of beings in their vital conditions with the strange features of nocturnal animals; a cyclopean eye, the whitened stare of larva, flying foxes wrapped in coats, prosimian spectres and lemurs, vampires and noctules. In order to produce these figures I would have needed not the rod of a glass-blower but the brush of a Hokusai, the demonic pencil of a Goya, the nightmares of an Odilon Redon....

The possibility of yet another image, newer still, presented itself at the unforgettable celebration at the Sorbonne: the same

---

*This description, which was delivered to Pasteur in manuscript form at the same time as the crystal goblet, was brought to the attention of the press. It first appeared in a daily newspaper and was later published in the *Revue encyclopédique,* May 15, 1893. Note: Pasteur's seventieth birthday was December 27, 1892

Rembrandtesque image came to the mind of two speakers. M. Charles Dupuy had qualified Pasteur's doctrine, the fertile doctrine of germs, as the "penetration of the mysterious depths of elementary nature" and M. Lister in turn declared: *O powerful beam of light that has illuminated the dark world of surgery !* Before them, Renan, marveling at your methods, had cast forth that phrase, magnificent as a meteor: *Luminous trail in the great night of the infinitely small, in the abyss of Being where Life is born.* Earlier still, however, Hugo had seen

The monstrous abyss filled with thick vapor Light up with starry beams.

He had already glimpsed the curiously inclined, despotically posed microscope

  Looking at the infinite form down below.

Here he has found a source of light that is shed forth onto the obscurity, projecting the new phantasmagoria of microbiological realities.

What the glassblower had thus dreamed of was throwing into the crucible that grand gesture of science, of making the very monsters themselves with their cursed masks float in the vitreous paste, of stripping the chimerical shreds, the hazy and specious hypotheses that you, Master, have reduced to nought. They have left their Stymphalus, exorcised by you, great conjurer of atoms!

This black crystal is but a paraphrase of the quasi-divine inspiration of Victor Hugo; and still, this chiseled version can hardly match the vision that the poet evokes:

One will see a herd of formidable Hydras Emerge, rising from the depths of unfathomable mists
    To be transfigured.

To be transfigured! How was one to trans-late plastically the metamorphosis of scientific errors like the doctrine of miasmata or spontaneous generation? I tried to show this through the representation of unreal beings, like the monsters that are formed by the clouds at sunset, as they meet with the observing eye – your luminous gaze, Master.

Before that ray of light they grow pale, tremble, and are distorted. Behind these transparent phantoms, one can see, interposed between the vitreous layers that were elaborated at great heat, the images of those *formidable Hydras,* those microbes, obscure instigators of great tragic works.

Here the stigmata of an imaginary Python become clear and obligingly assume, in their characteristic form, the decorative pattern of a bacteria deadly to us. Elsewhere the stretched and streaky form of a fantastic pterodactyl enclosed in light is fragmented into *neat little square* articles; this is to suggest the nature of Pasteur's *gas bacillus.*

Thus it is that beneath the visionary anatomies we may decipher the realities that you have uncovered, ordered, cataloged, and cultured in test tubes. Given the fragility of the tiny models and a lack of training in this kind of presentation – for this goblet is unique and there is no other – these figures must seem decidedly crude. But the art of evocation thrives on semblance; how much more suggestive is the image than the imitation!

Beneath the amber colored penumbra lie scattered dim black reminders of a chicken languishing away, of a sinister dog foaming at the mouth, fixed emblems of the causalities that you, Master, in your glory knew how to unravel, just as you proved the relation to their respective effects: the virus swimming among globules of blood, germs carried off into the atmosphere, the elegant sporulations of the *Saccharomyces Pastorianus*, the symmetrical constriction of the bacteria in your *micrococcus cholerae gallinarum* as they are split in two, that also of the dreaded *Pasteur micrococcus*, the spirilla of stagnant water, the decorative parasite of malarial infections, the *pneumonia staphylococcus*, the coloration of the *violet bacillus*. Forms that are shaped like a weaver's shuttle or like a rosary; the whitish *colonies of cultures on plate*.

Inside the vase, the branches, rootlets, or barbs of gathered feathers try to imitate the development of certain cultures injected into gelatin. The shade of yellow is a mistake; however, that is due to the inaccuracy of a defective chromolithograph in a manual. These various figurations maintain their curiosity in the art of glass. Everything leads one to suppose that the fearful nature of these symbols will keep their respective alchemies, unrivaled by imitation. As it is, you see for yourself that *fin de siècle* crystal is incapable of matching your art in capturing the intangible. Our art has not that long tenacity of spirit nor as much ingenious originality nor personal invention.

However we look at it, Master, your followers would be right to judge this "innoculated" glass unsatisfactory were it to suggest only – and rather inadequately at that – the experimental proof of the Pasteur doctrine of germs.

Were that the case, it would provide a poor response indeed to the profound feelings of the Ecole Normale and to the great honor done to a glass artist, if the worker had not known how to add another and more moving aspect to the glorious one. To be sure, the glass artist knows full well that the crowning achievement of your research is the effective relief it has provided. We all know that for millions of human lives, victims of obscure scourges, you were born too late: "Had you been there, my brother Lazarus would not have died." But here you are at long last! How then could the artist possibly avoid the tender filial devotion that has filled the hearts of your students and commanded our unanimous gratitude forever? And thus, the engraver's tool released white tears of a soothing balm to flow over those bleeding thorns of pain, and over the open wounds of men and animals, the balm of pity, your pity,

> All the pity that Thou hast
> planted in the heart.

How dated all this seems for your art, Master – these old symbols of modern antisepsis and the vaccines that offer suffering the hope and certainty of a cure, that bestow upon you "the love that stems from grief"!

That too is a phrase from Victor Hugo.

Seeing as how he, the great visionary, foresaw it all, they are his words that are inscribed on the other side of the Pasteur Coupe.

> I move about in meditation,
> And at all moments a certain instinct
> obliges me
> To seek and find what lies behind
> the suffering of men.

It was the belief of the glass artist, and your friends have agreed with him, that with this the poet offers his pure homage to your kind and charitable genius.

May this cooled crystal thus preserve the reflection of your flame along with the ardor of the fine youth of France and may it be a token of the respect, the sincerity, and the tenderness that has inspired this homage as well as this work! (*Ecrits* pp. 148-154.)

5a) **Magnolia**

5) MAGNOLIA

...the closest white to the heart of a magnolia blossom, with the translucencies of jade;... (*Ecrits*, p. 174)

DEPICTED ON THE VASE are magnolia branches and blossoms in early spring, before the leaves appear. It is enameled inside as well as outside, with the white on the interior. Branches and buds are engraved.

The work illustrates an interesting attitude toward contours. Rigidly delineated, "anemic" blossoms in white enamel are diffused by soft colors with very low contrast edges. These are described by Gallé: "...where the gold precipitate has marked the sodium based glass with spots of blue, violet, currant-red, chestnut brown, and earthy brown; this effect is meant to imitate the colors of the scales and petals that curl about the buds and blossoms of the magnolia." (*Ecrits*, p. 339). The mystery of the whole is further enhanced by random bubbles floating through the glass like crystal balls and tiny nebulae of blue spots surrounding gold centers.

In detail 5b, notice how the deeply engraved bud and twig diffuse the white enamel behind it. The duality so evident in Gallé's work (as with the two dragonflies on the coupe, 23) appears here too: enamel bud, under engraved bud, separated forever by a thickness of glass.

Date: 1889 · H. 22.4 cm, D. (rim) 14 cm
Blown; patination; enameled; engraved; some gilt surfaces.
Signed (on base): *E. Gallé fecit Nanceus No 166* and *E194*
Collection: Musée des Arts Décoratifs, Paris, No. 5670
Exhibited at the 1889 Paris Universal Exposition

6a) **Meadow Heracleum**

6) MEADOW HERACLEUM

IN THE 1870S AND EIGHTIES, Gallé experimented extensively with enamels on glass. Many of the resulting works had themes of historic precedent: mosque lamps, ancient Egyptian motifs, etc. Some, such as the Magnolia of 1889 (5), depict subjects faithfully drawn from the study of nature.

By 1900 Gallé's style had matured with works like Thistles (12) and Violet (18), but *this* vase reminds us that his interest in enamels persisted. It is a pastiche of influences: the Japanese style landscape (6b) with its predictable lines and clouds anticipates Art Deco designs, while leaves on the front (6a) form an abstract design in an Arabic sense (top), like Gothic shields (bottom), and in the spirit of the Baroque (center). The prominent asterisk-shaped forms near the top are the umbells of the Meadow Heracleum. Characteristic of Gallé, the piece illustrates both symmetry and the breaking of symmetry, with some leaves healthy, vital, and straight, others dying and curled.

Dated 1900 · H. 45.1 cm, D. (max) 21.5 cm; D. (rim) 14.6 cm
Blown (probably in an optic mold); acid-etched; enameled; gilt
Signed: *Gallé 1900*
Collection: Musée de L'Ecole de Nancy, Nancy, France

7a) Vase in reflected light

7b) **Vase in transmitted light**

7) AUTUMN

VARIOUS DEAD AUTUMN LEAVES are represented, and although different plants can produce leaves which *seem* to be similar, the large central leaf (7a) is probably maple, while the triangular-shaped leaf in the detail (7c) looks like Colt's foot.

The vase has two distinctly different appearances: in reflected light, we are aware of the engraved leaves, some picked out with touches of smoky blue edging; in transmitted light, we see ghostly amber forms where the leaves were. Dark leech or pterodactyl-like shapes—unrelated to the leaf patterns—dominate. Are these leaves seen on edge through dappled forest light? Even in reflected light, transmission occurs as light reflects from internal bits of metal foil (7c).

Autumn reminds us that Gallé uses his glass as though it were a painter's canvas, but with several advantages. Curved surfaces permit disappearance while leading the eye around to other viewing points. Primary and secondary views (e.g., front, main view; back, subject of lesser importance) may be developed. While most canvases act as impermeable surfaces onto which pigment is applied, Gallé's "canvas," the glass wall of the vessel, can act as a framework on which decoration is almost literally hung (Orchids [19]), or decoration may protrude (the Dragonfly Coupe [23]). In Autumn, decoration may appear to be flat on the surface, but on inspection (in transmitted light) it is revealed as a visibly thick form imbedded within the glass (the dark internal inclusions).

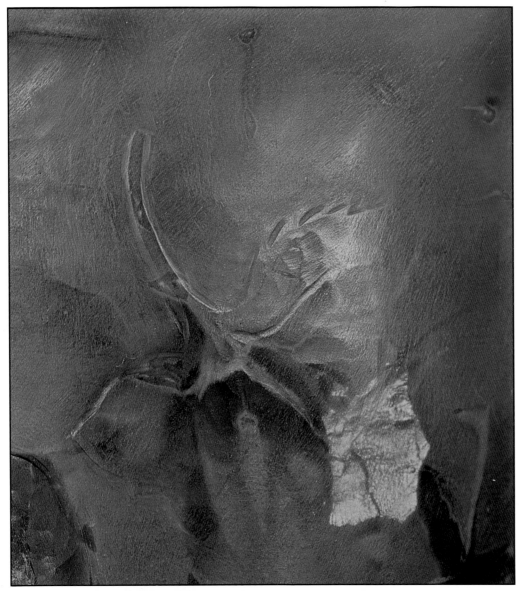

7c) Detail showing leaf at upper left

Date: About 1900 · H. 16.9 cm, D. (rim) 9.2 cm
Blown; dark internal inclusions and metallic foil; probably fumed blue-white surfaces; engraved.
Signed (above base): *Gallé*
Collection: Musée des Arts Décoratifs, Paris, No. 19649; previously in the Roger Marx collection (#83 in the Roger Marx Auction, 1914)

8a) Forest and Wildflowers

8) FOREST AND WILDFLOWERS

The poetic impression is freed, at least for those who know the beauty of night, and who cherish the somewhat disconcerting darkness of a night in the forest, the vague distress which takes unawares the walker who finds himself in the evening, at the edge of the woods. There, strange lights hover in the darkness, the rustle, the whispering and mysterious activity of things which are unseen, but which watch, and go about their business in secret.

Emile Gallé (*Ecrits*, pp. 205-266)

8b) Side left of 8a

8c) Detail of 8b

AGAINST A BACKGROUND OF TREES float four-petaled flowers, possibly pink or white dogwood (*Cornus*); a less likely possibility is evening primrose (*Oenotheria*). The former is associated with early spring, the latter with late summer.

The innermost layer of the bowl is pinkish, engraved away in places to depict clouds behind the engraved trees which are amber-brown. By fuming the exterior surface, shiny cold highlights on the flowers turn into veils of blue and lavender, elegant foils for the ambers and pinks transmitted through the translucent parts. As in Joan of Arc (3), the juxtaposition of warm and cool colors results in a dramatic division of space as the floral "bouquets" float in the foreground, a great distance in front of the forest. The effect is of a far-off wood at twilight.

Date: About 1895-1900 · H. 14.5 cm, D. (max) 24 cm
Blown; overlays; possibly acid-etched; cut and engraved; fumed surface
Signed (near base): *Gallé*
Collection: Private

9a) Iris

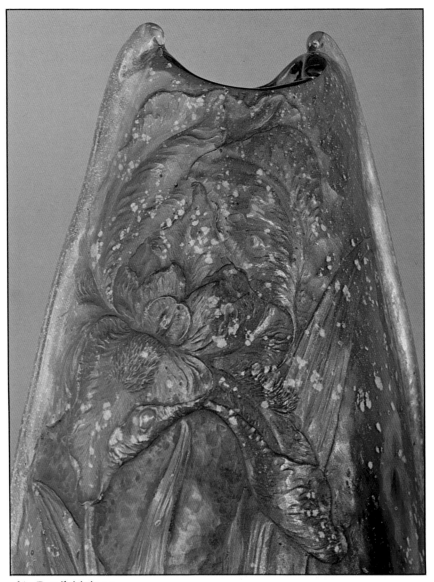

9b) Detail, iris in 9a

9) IRIS

Indeed, love of nature must always lead to symbolism: the popular flower loved by all will always occupy a principal role in ornamental symbolism. Gutskow tells the story of a man who set off in quest of true happiness. He questioned a flower who sent him to see a star. The star in turn replied to the man: 'Hurry back to the cornflower.'

Emile Gallé (*Ecrits*, p. 218)

9c) Reverse side

9d) Detail, wilted iris in 9c

THIS IS A VASE that begs to be handled! Photographs can only show it as sooty and somewhat malformed. At close range, it is like a starry night, the front engraved with a bearded iris (also known as a fleur-de-lis, 9b). With a little imagination the black background, covered with flecks that look like bits of old newspaper becomes a night sky brilliant with light. Gallé's story reminds us of this vase, for we as viewers move back and forth between the flower and the stars – encouraged by Gallé who uses the transparency of glass to create a ghostly image: we see *through* the flower (9b). In the process, a subtle relationship between background and flower is established when this background appears to lie on *top* of the iris.

On the reverse, overlaid with tints of orange and ultramarine and also engraved (9d), is a wilted iris. The overall form, edged with bubbly colorless glass, is similar in shape to the Philadelphia Dragonfly vase (24).

Date: About 1895-1900 · H. 32.7 cm, W. (max) 15.5 cm
Blown; cased; possibly marquetry inlays or trailing and staining; internal patination; cut, engraved; on bronze base
Signed: (on leaf above the base on blossoming iris side) *Gallé*
Collection: Private

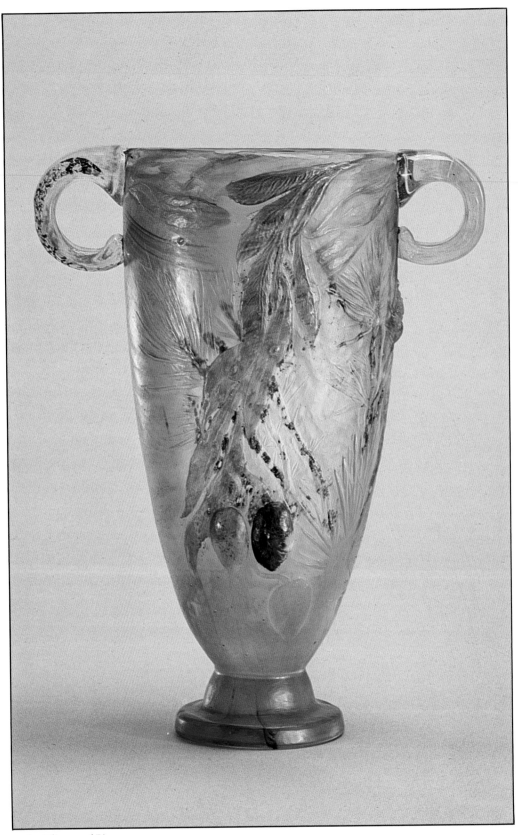

10a) Olives and Pines

10) OLIVES AND PINES

To the simple contours of the vase are etched...the mosaic of your cones, o woodland pines! Your gemstones of matte flowers blossom, shaped out of topaz and amber pastes amid the feathers of your sharpening flowers. With an impulse which every attack of the surly wind only renders more nervous, your branch rises, and goes to marry itself for love to the olive tree up there, the olive tree, radiant bride of silver, which leans over, soon drooping with the weight of its olives, modeled out of crystal the color of savory nephrite.

Emile Gallé (*Ecrits*, p. 184)

SO GALLÉ DESCRIBED THE GIFT, similar in form and decoration to the Olives and Pines vase, which he made for his good friend Victor Prouvé in 1896. As befits its subject of pines and olives, it is a classic shape; in the essay cited above, Gallé calls the vase a cantharus (drinking cup with handles).

Notice the three olives on one face and the pair of olives on the opposite side: in each case, one unripe (green) and one ripe (black) olive, and in the grouping of three, a "ghost" olive is engraved. The olive leaves are colored by a scummy green patination and textured with bubbles, both beneath a transparent layer of glass. A cinder-like black patina emphasizes the pine branches, which are also given texture with bubbles; these bubbles, and the young, reddish, probably female pine cones (ready for pollination) are visible in illustration 10b. The handles of the vase are different—one colorless, one yellow. In the Prouvé vase, a symbolic meaning was given to each handle; "one of which still seems red from the fire of the oven, and the other, iridescent with the apotheosis which fills us with joy, that of our comrade (Prouvé) who has labored so long." (*Ecrits*, p. 183.)

In many instances, Gallé prefers pairings, dualities: two olives, in two stages of development; three-dimensional olives and an engraved, two-dimensional one; olives and pines—which grow in the same terrain. The dualism may indicate time's passage: youth to old age, unripe to ripe, etc. Other objects with details that appear in two ways include the Dragonfly Coupe (23), Autumn (7), and Barley (14). By giving a subject existence on two planes, the commitment to either is lessened, and the idea transcends its representation, a characteristic of symbolism. Gallé also preferred variations on a given theme; besides this and the Prouvé vase, similar designs were made, including "No more War, No more Blood," ("Plus de Guerre, Plus de Sang" after Victor Hugo),* and "Eruption," (L'Eruption).**

Date: About 1896-1904 · H. 24.3 cm., W. (max.) 19.7 cm, D. (base) 7.3 cm
Blown; patination; applied bits (handles and olives); engraved.
Signed: *Gallé,* below rim to right of the two uppermost olives.
Collection: Private

* Illustrated, p. 41, *Emile Gallé,* Louis de Fourcaud, Paris: Librarie de L'Art, 1903.
** Number 3 in the Exposition de L'Ecole de Nancy, Paris, Pavillon de Marsan, 1903.

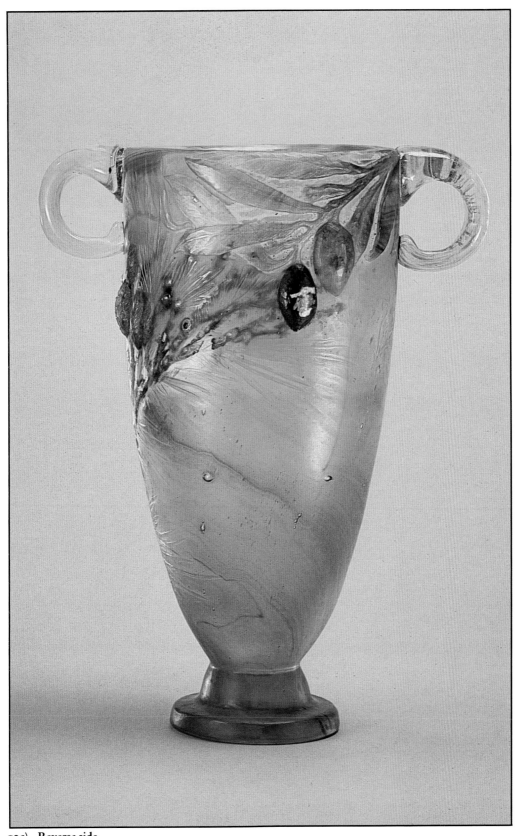

10c) **Reverse side**

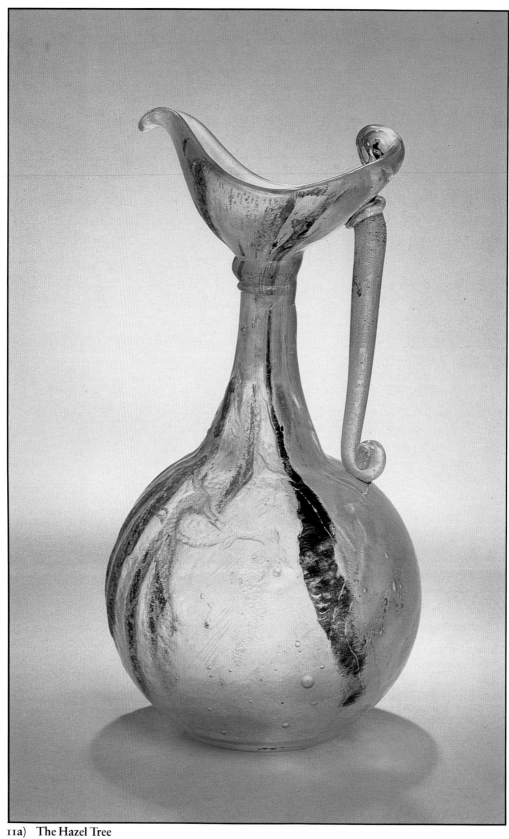

11a) The Hazel Tree

11) THE HAZEL TREE

Clear crystal ewer, agatized by oxidation, with iridescent re-
fraction and purpurine transparencies. The engraving sus-
pends the flower of the nut tree in all its nuances to the pouch
which is beaded with blonde reflections. Pollen spreads a
sulfurous cloud on the ruby stigmata and future hazelnuts. The
anxiety of inflorescences, whorls and pendants becomes
windblown in the rude awakening of February. The oblique
sleet, the blue-tinged rainbowed vapors, melt on the branches
which drip into liquid pustulas, in rippling tears of crystal: first
laughter of the year, uncertain hope, premature decoration.
    Not with pearls embroidered,
    but with all my tears. *

Emile Gallé (*Ecrits*, pp.160-161.)

* The quotation at the end is from Baudelaire, "To a Madonna"

11b) Reverse side

11c) Detail of 11b

THE PIECE HAS A CURIOUS ARCHITECTURE, as if based on a confusion or pastiche of forms borrowed from ancient vessels. Notice the handle, which seems to be intended more to support the flared lip than for holding; its base ends in a spiral which turns back on itself (11c).

The Hazel Tree is a good example of the tactile quality of Gallé's work. Most of the surface decoration is subtle, dependent upon changing conditions of light for its effect (the blonde reflections of the beaded "pouch" are dichroic, and thus become "purpurine transparencies" in transmitted light). It is through *handling* the piece that one makes the best acquaintance with its characteristics; unfortunately, most of us can only *look* at such works! Another example of a "tactile" work is Deep Sea (36).

Dated 1893 · H. 21.9 cm, D. (max.) 11.6 cm
Blown; patination; metal flecks; engraved.
Signed (on base): *E* (Cross of Lorraine) *Gallé* [fecit?] *1893*
Inscribed: *Non de perles brodé, mais de toutes mes larmes*
Collection: Private

12a) Thistles

12) THISTLES

...we are fully aware that the eloquence of a flower, thanks to the mysteries of its organism and destiny, thanks to the synthesis of the botanical symbol that is achieved by the pencil of the artist, often surpasses the authority of the human figure in the intensity of its suggestive power. We know that the expression in our own heraldic thistle, for instance, relates to a defiant gesture...

Emile Gallé (*Ecrits*, p. 216)

THE OVERALL FORM OF THE VASE, created by mold blowing, is of the cone and bracts (modified leaves) of an unopened thistle. The thistle is a symbol of the region of Lorraine and hence of the city of Nancy (which was the capital of the duchy of Lorraine); it was used frequently as a patriotic symbol by Gallé. The flange protruding at the right (12a) – which was caused by hot glass pushing out through the seam of the mold – suggests one of the long leaves of a thistle. Depicted *on* the vase (12b) is a mature thistle; the purple at the top is the cotton: silky hairs which carry the seeds away. The decoration, representing a mature thistle, overlays the form, which is a young thistle, as if two separate objects were trying to occupy the same space. This idea of decoration as an equal, or even dominant, partner of form is just the reverse of the Bauhaus (a school established 1919 in Germany, noted for its emphasis on austere, functional design) seccessionists, etc. In fact, "more is more" seems to characterize Gallé's approach, where form is frequently *determined* by the decoration. Notice details such as the use of a molding spur – which most glassmakers would polish away or hide.

Here nature appears in a light shed uniquely by Gallé: a world of green, sky of blue changing to pink amber where the thistle – all gray, mauve, rose, and lavender – rises. It is in what amber does to pink, brown to black (see Joan of Arc, 3) green to blue, that his special style stands out – not with the primary colors and their opposites. Every hue contains traces of every other.

The transition of one color to another or one form to another offers a range of possibilities from the abrupt (like the color shifts in national flags) to the subtle, barely perceptible (like the elusive line where the pink stops and the blue begins in a sky just after sundown). Gallé's edges are remarkable for their transitions. For example, the thistle, including its leaves, is hard-edged, often with a contrasting line in color lying wire-like around a field of color (12a, the leaves at the base). Meanwhile, the blue curve extending *over* the thistle from the mold spur blends its color with the underlying reds and greens in a range of varying color and thicknesses. Gallé's preference for threatening edges (collars of spikes) is also evident. Perhaps the role of these edges is twofold: first, to establish mood; second, to change subject (spikes are inherent in thistles) into symbol (spikes of defiance).

12b) Detail

Date 1900 · H. 44.5 cm, D. (rim) 18 cm
Mold-blown; overlays; marquetry inlays.
Signed: *Gallé*
Collection: Musée des Arts Décoratifs, Paris, France, #9363
Exhibited: Paris Universal Exposition 1900

13a) Geology

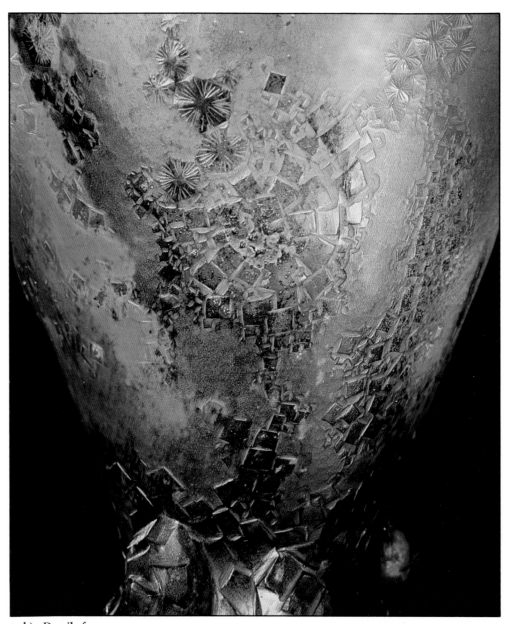

13b) Detail of 13a

13) GEOLOGY

THE VASE SEEMS TO REPRESENT the growth of crystals either inside pockets in rocks (geodes) or in caverns as a stalagmite formation. Drops of liquid (13c) near the top, with carbonates in solution, become fully developed crystals near the base. The starburst flakes (13b) may be associated with malachite (a source of copper), while the rhomboids (also 13b) are typical of calcite. Streaks of blue may be azurite.

Gallé's sensitivity to color is apparent in the subtle surprises that lie in the colors themselves, in their pairing, in their location – for example, on closer inspection, flecks of red (13b) where only black and turquoise, gold and silver are at first perceived.

This vase and the majority of works illustrated have an aspect of preciousness. Geology appears to be made of rare and rich materials, carefully worked with extraordinary skill. Yet we know that glass was cheap and that the craftsmanship is not extraordinary by the standards of the time. Could it be the *memory* of other things that each piece evokes? In handling Geology, our experience with rock crystal, malachite, and azurite obliterates their reality: although they are *glass* imitations, we regard them as prized stones.

Gallé is never a decorator: his pictorial matter usually does *not* fit conveniently within the panels, friezes, sides, and shoulders of his pieces – his subject matter transcends his forms. But there are many situations in which the form or shape come into existence through the subject matter itself (for example, Thistles 12). In Geology the ring of crystals becomes a wide-flaring knop in a classical shape.

As in vases such as Tadpoles (32), the artist here evokes a sense of metamorphosis, an element of time passing; liquid drops become solid crystals. Gallé thrives in this element of suspended time when nature is in slow transition. Geology reminds us once again of the role in Gallé's work played by the glassy matrix itself. It reads like his personal firmament, a material of infinite depth in which what we see on the surface may indeed appear again and again, huge or tiny with limitless space a psychological, if not intellectual, goal.

Date: About 1900-1904 · H. 24.9 cm, D. (max) 11.5 cm, D. (base) 11.1 cm
Signed (above base): *Gallé*
Blown; internal patination; applied bits; cut, engraved. In two parts (joint above knop).
Collection: Musée de l'Ecole de Nancy, Nancy, France

13c) Reverse side

14a) **Barley**

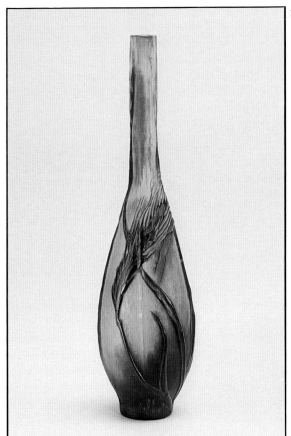

14) BARLEY

THE VASE REPRESENTS BARLEY, with the lower stalk (14a) wilted. The vitality of nature so suffuses Gallé's life and work that he cannot tolerate the specimen alone. He sees the complete cycle from bud to dry curling death, for even on this simple vase he portrays two stalks of barley, one vital, one in decline.

If the Grape bottle (15) is among Gallé's most flamboyant shapes, Barley is among his most restrained. The plants seem integrated into the ovoid, long-necked silhouette; where the engraved surfaces break the edges (the left shoulder in 14a) the sensation is delicately tactile—there's an impulse to run the hand over them. A molded, vertical gully bisects the center (14a) and is echoed on the reverse side (14b) by a *raised* ridge. The engraved barley rising up on the neck (14a), appears only as a reddish, diffused blotch from the opposite side (14b), touchable on one side, untouchable on the other.

Date: About 1902-1904 · H. 32.8 cm, W. 8.9 cm
Blown in a mold; overlays; cut, engraved.
Signed (near base): *Gallé*
Collection: Private; previously, Roger Marx (#100 in the Roger Marx auction, 1914)

15a) Grapes

15) GRAPES

Wine can endow the lowest dive
*   with sudden luxury*
and out of a red mist create
*   enchanted porticoes*
like sunset firing a sodden sky.
(inscription on the bottle)
"Poison," Charles Baudelaire; trans. Richard Howard,
    Les Fleurs du Mal, Boston: Godine, 1982, p. 54

THE BOTTLE REPRESENTS GRAPES, tendrils, and leaves; the stopper probably represents the vapor of wine referred to in the poem, which is inscribed below the shoulder (15b). Different types of grapes for making wine are depicted (stained, or colored in the mass of the glass: green, red, purple, colorless, and yellow, some backed with metal foil for brilliance), but in nature they would not be growing from the same vines as they are here—and grapes grow in bunches, not singly.

It is certainly one of Gallé's most striking shapes, with the regular architecture of the bottle and its handle acting as a foil: the grapes break its profile; the "steam stopper," all frozen curves, rises above. A clever idea—a stopper (whose function is to contain) is made to look like it is not doing its duty, but in fact *becomes* what it contains.

Gallé applies his inscriptions and signatures with infinite variety; in this case they form a skin on the surface like theatrical scrim or the credits at a movie which appear to float in front of the action. This reflects the contradictory, enigmatic nature of Gallé, who puts an idea (expressed by someone else) on the surface while his ideas surround and *back up* words.

Dated 1900 · H. (overall) 32.5 cm (approx); W. (max) 12.6 cm
Blown (possibly mold-blown); overlay; foil inclusions; possibly
trailed decoration and applied bits; stained; cut, engraved.
Signed: *Emile Gallé/1900*
Inscribed (on one side): *Le vin sait revètir le plus sordide bouge*
　　　　　　　　　　　　D'un luxe miraculeux,
　　　　　　　　　　　　Et fait surgir plus d'un portique fabuleux
　　　　　　　　　　　　Dans l'or de sa vapeur rougx,
　　　　　　　　　　　　Comme un soleil couchant
　　　　　　　　　　　　dans un ciel nébuleux　　　*Baudelaire*

Collection: Private

15b) **Reverse side with inscription**

16a) **Landscape**

16) LANDSCAPE

TREE TRUNKS WITH STUMPS of branches encircle a field with houses. In the foreground are forms suggesting rocks or undergrowth. One tree has fallen over.

In many of Gallé's pieces, heavy applied decoration has some effect on the supporting form; for example, orchids seem to split forms apart (19 and 20). Here, tree trunks act like jailhouse bars, framing the landscape within. If we think of the piece in full round, we realize that the forest has encircled the entire landscape, sky and all. This landscape takes on a geological, stratified appearance accentuated by the trees which intersect the "layers" (green grass, blue sky, etc.) at sharp angles.

Date: About 1900 · H. 21.8 cm; D. (max.) 16.7 cm
Blown; multiple overlays; marquetry inlays; applied bits; patination.
Signed (on base): *Gallé*
Collection: Private

17a) **Rhubarb**

17) RHUBARB

THE OVERALL FORM REPRESENTS a convoluted leaf, while the engraved landscape on one side (see especially details 17c and d) depicts the entire plant, probably with its reflection in water. Illustrated in the catalog for the 1903 Exposition de l'Ecole de Nancy, it is called *La Feuille de Rhubarbe*.

As in the Thistles (12), the overall form of the vessel and its decoration represent different aspects of the same plant. This, along with such pieces as the small Pines vase (21) and Sea Horses (34), is one of Gallé's "invented" shapes: not quite like anything man-made *or* anything natural. Nonetheless, it is recognizable as a vessel form – the applied leaves make the base, while the turning of the great leaf establishes itself as a handle.

The marquetry inlay, which has been "corroded" by engraving, is especially visible in transmitted light (detail 17d) where it appears as an inverted triangular shape with its apex cut away. Comparison with detail 17c reveals the multiple existences of Gallé's glasses, each depending upon the ratio of reflected to transmitted light (17c has much more reflected light than 17d). In general, Gallé seems to have intended his works to be seen in both kinds of light simultaneously.

As on pieces like Thistles (12), decoration so dominates that it determines form; in the process, functional shapes are eroded, while edges (rims, spouts, bases) become occasions for interesting silhouettes and encourage subject recognition (the curved edge of a leaf, the scalloped edge of a pine cone or a blossom).

17b) **Reverse side**

Date: About 1903 · H. 21.1 cm, W. 31.5 cm
Blown; marquetry inlays; applied bits; patination; cut, engraved. In two parts (base un-
screws).
Signed (below landscape): *Gallé*
Collection: Private
Exhibited: Exposition de l'Ecole de Nancy, Pavillon de Marsan, Paris 1903

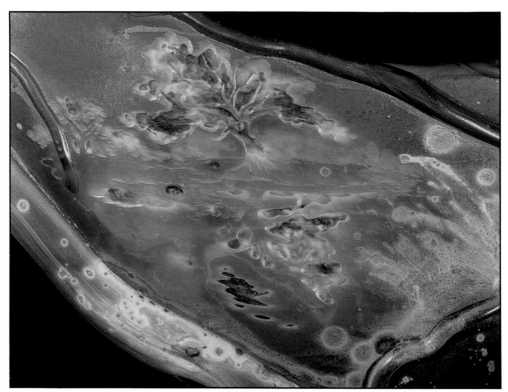

17c) Detail of 17b in transmitted and reflected light

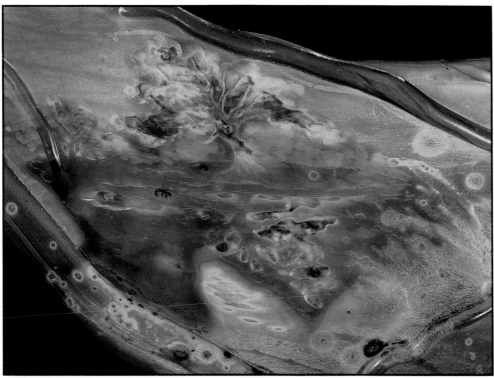

17d) Detail of 17b in predominantly transmitted light

18a) Violet

18) VIOLET

GALLÉ'S SPRING VIOLET has leaves on the base which point down. While the general form is reminiscent of the treatment of the Rhubarb coupe (17), it is more regular and was mold-blown. As with the Thistle vase (12) and the Rhubarb coupe, the overall form and the applied decoration represent different aspects of the same plant.

The variety of textures, as much to be felt as seen, is exceptional: smooth, fresh from the mold surfaces (base and bulbous form at the left of illustration 18); internal network of veining – easy to see, impossible to touch – near the "spout" (the left side of the illustration); fat bubbles under the applied leaves (center of the illustration, above the knop) easy to touch, hard to see (a similar surface is achieved in Deep Sea [36]).

Dated: 1900 · H. 23.3 cm, D. (base) 12.6 cm
Mold-blown; internal and surface patination; marquetry; cut, engraved.
Signed: (on one leaf/stem on base): *Expos. 1900* and *Gallé;* paper sticker under base:
CRISTALLERIE D'EMILE GALLE MARQUE DEPOSEE NANCY
surrounding *E* (Cross of Lorraine) *G.*
Collection: Private
Exhibited: Probably Paris Universal Exposition 1900

19a) Orchids

19b) Reverse side

19, 20) ORCHIDS (two vases)

*Tell me, do the very orchids of Crousse, the eminent grower,
those jewels of pure freshness, of pleasant peculiarity, of
stranger wonder,* Brassia bicolor, *its reseda-green scratched
with Indian ink,* Cochlyodes *where the coral and the brightest
scarlet fade under a spark of unexpected blue, somber* Laelia,
sly Cypripedium, *fluttering of* Oncidium, *all moving like oc-
topi perceived under the water of an aquarium, flowers grown
indifferent to the cries of ecstasy and the 'Oh! Mama,'—possess
the philter flowing from the blue gaze of the periwinkles?*

Emile Gallé (*Ecrits,* p. 80)

THE TWO VASES (19 and 20) display orchids, one rather realistically portrayed (19), the other more stylized (20). The life cycle of a flower is traced from vibrant blossoms (front) to languid, drooping leaves and blossoms (back). We have also noted Gallé's theme of time's passage in Thistles (12), Geology (13), Barley (14), Iris (9), Tadpoles (32). Heavy applied decoration seems to burst the sustaining vessels apart, the opposite of Landscape (16) with its enclosing trees.

Flamboyant hotworking techniques are used to model the blossoms—especially the pink Orchid (19). The raised flowers are subtly melded with the supporting surfaces and to each other through engraving. Near the applied, three-dimensional Orchid (19) is an emerging, ghost-like, "flat" engraved one. The piece becomes a garden floating in space, with some flowers bursting out, some falling back into deep space, another example of the duality that seems so characteristic of Gallé.

(19)
Dated: 1900 · H. 23 cm, W. (max.) 14.2 cm
Blown; overlay; applications; cut, engraved
Signed (on side): *Gallé/1900*
Inscribed (on base): *affection*
Collection: Private; originally Roger Marx (No. 98 in the Roger Marx auction, 1914)

19c)   Side left of 19a

20a) **Orchid**

20b) Reverse side

(20)
Date: About 1900 · H. 22.5 cm, W. (max.) 14.3
Blown; internal patina; applications; fumed surfaces; cut, engraved
Signed (above base): *Gallé*
Collection: Private

21a) Pines

21, 22) PINES (two vases)

...it is a shape of calm energy, of simple power; it is free and natural art which neither disdains, envies or borrows. Grown without any stable fertilizer, from solitudes and austerities, it yields its balsamic greenness, in the winter as in the spring. It offers its slender trunk clothed with a squamous dress, of geometric design, of sand-pink color, to the thoughts of the architect. To schools it offers studies of its branches, the gestures of its wrestler's arms, models filled with character and grace.

Emile Gallé (*Ecrits*, The Prouvé Vase, p. 184)

21b) Side left of 21a

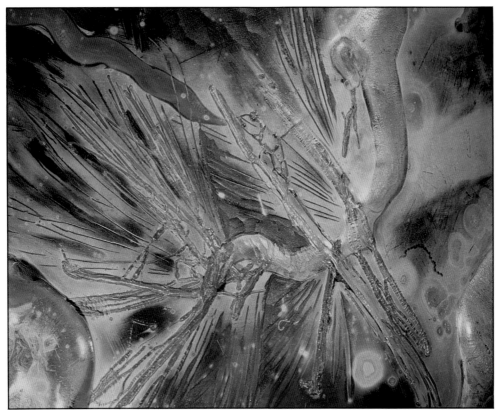

21c) Detail showing needles at bottom of 21d

THE PINE TREE IS OFTEN USED by Gallé for its powerful symbolism. But are the heavy applications on the vases really meant to be pine cones? If anything, they look more like bunches of grapes, pitted cinders, or deflated balloons.

A comparison of decorative elements shared by both pieces reveals how Gallé subtly varied his themes. The applied bits encircling the tops and bottoms of each vase are probably meant to be pine cone scales. In the large vase they are bent at the ends and look a little like dolphin snouts, although in general they retain a liquid look as though hot and reminiscent of the glass made by Louis C. Tiffany in America at about the same time to imitate molten lava. Here Gallé is concerned with a straightforward, if perhaps oversimplified, botanical detail. However, in the smaller vase Gallé shifts his intent. A number of applied scales have a wet look, but engraving reveals some blue and white interiors (21b, base). Perhaps the intent is to reduce the three-dimensional to the two-dimensional; the last two scales at the top (right side of 21e) are only sketchy engraved lines against the patinated background. Again, we see the duality of images typical of Gallé (as in the applied and ghost dragonflies in 23).

21d) Side right of 21a

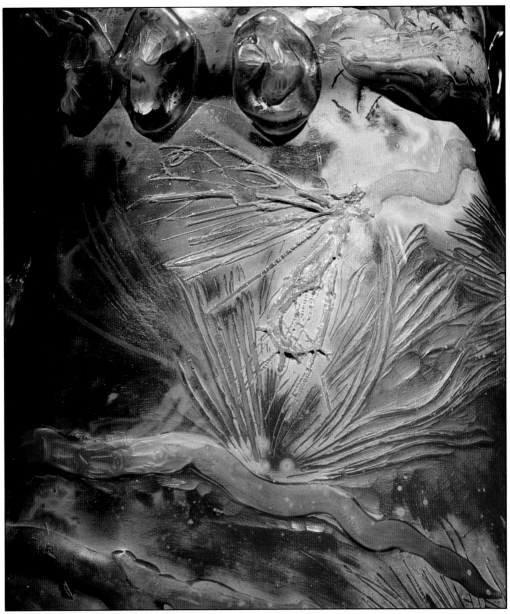

21e) Detail showing needles at top of 21d

The pine needles are also different in each piece. The large vase has many needles, and they fan out freely into space (22c); the transition from branch to needles is effected with an intervening, pinkish cone-like form. In the small vase, the needles seem cramped for space – they don't fan out but overlap or turn back on themselves (21e). On this somewhat "frantic" surface we miss the graceful transition between branch and needles – here they project randomly from the ends of the branches or even run on top of the branches. In both vases, needles are embedded within the body of the glass itself (21e, 22c). In the smaller piece, the transition from outside to inside has more gradations: needles as applied threads, partly engraved threads, patina engraved as needles, needles trapped in glass as in amber. The congested surfaces of this little vase are extraordinary. In one detail (21c), along with the different treatments of needles, we have bursts of yellow gold patina like supernovae, a limb that goes from slightly raised and patinated (upper right) to heavily engraved (center), and a second branch (upper left) with a wiry black outline – reminding us of the diversity of edges achieved by Gallé. Of course there are the curious graffiti – to enrich the surface on an almost subliminal level – such as the squiggly inverted u-shape to the right of the central branch.

(21)
Dated: 1903 · H. 17.9 cm; W. (max.) 15.1. cm
Blown; marquetry; applied bits; patina; engraved
Signed (on pine cone scales above base): *Gallé* and *1903*
Collection: Private

(22)
Date: About 1902-1903 · H. 43.2 cm; D. (max.) 18 cm
Blown; marquetry; applied bits; patina; engraved
Signed (above base): *Gallé*. Paper label on base COLLECTION/ROGER MARX
Collection: Private, previously Roger Marx collection.

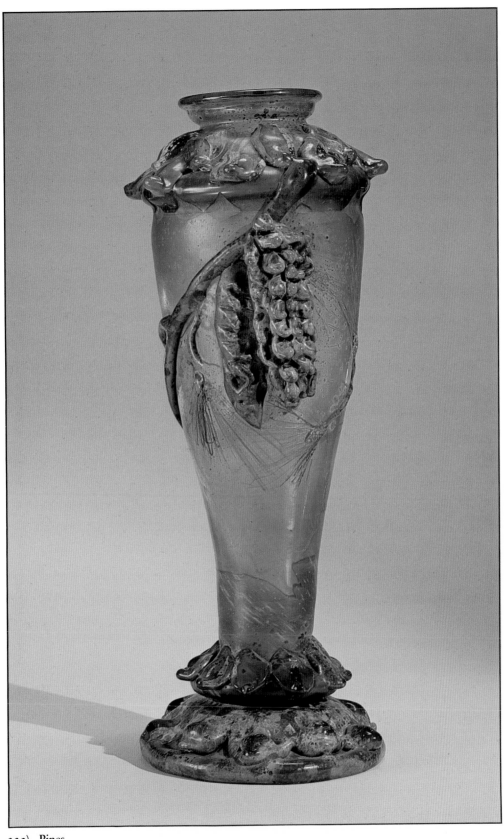

22a) Pines

22b) Side right of 22a

22c) Detail of needles in 22b

22d)   Side left of 22a

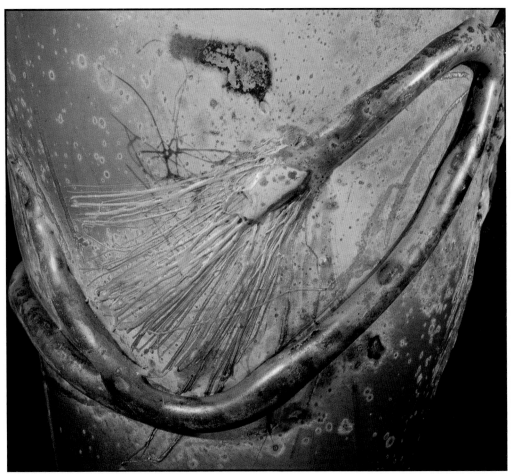

22e) Detail of needles in 22d

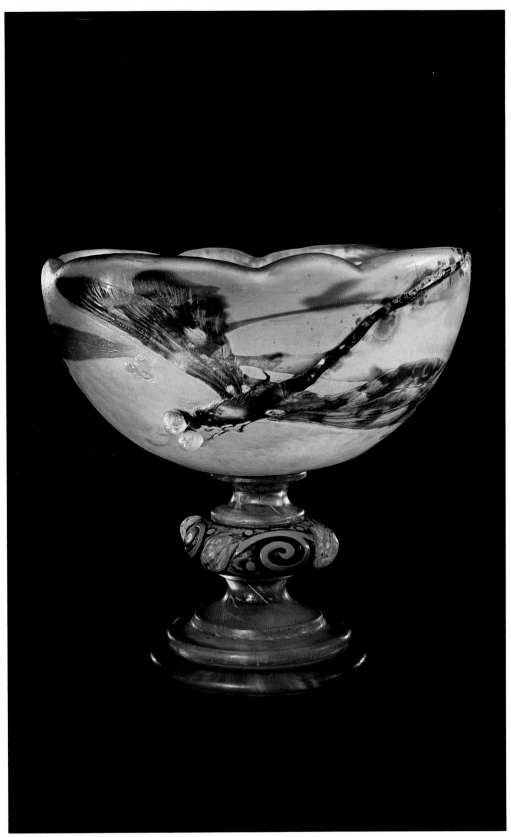

23a) **Dragonfly Coupe**

23b) Detail showing heads of insects on 23a

23) DRAGONFLY COUPE

GALLÉ'S REALISM is often difficult to gauge, as is the extent to which it was offset by artistic license and technical considerations. We know, for example, that Gallé was fond of the dragonfly motif (see the Philadelphia vase, 24), but the insect on this object more closely resembles an ant lion (order *Neuroptera*) with its long antennae and mottled brown wings. In one place Gallé even writes about "...the winged flutterings of a Neuroptera, ..." (*Ecrits*, p. 257). Perhaps our observation rests on a technical mistake, and the antennae are really legs that slipped during the forming process.

The piece has an architectural foot, but sandwiched in the middle is a cameo-engraved knop. The translucent gray and white appliqués attached to its surface are somewhat enigmatic. Are they unopened buds? If so, could the white cameo spiral be a stem? Supported by the classic foot and pseudo-classic knop (including a spiral which suggests classicism) is a bowl which is organic at the lip (the lobes suggest a flower). Once again, Gallé indicates his tendency to transform the man-made to the natural (see also Geology, 13).

On the center of the bowl is a large insect, partly applied to the surface (the eyes and segmented body with speckles of patina), partly beneath the surface (the mottling of the wings, the legs, "antennae"); the structure of the wings is detailed by engraving. Imbedded bits of silver-colored foil float in front of or near the wing (left of the bowl). To the left of this creature is a "ghost" image, identifiable on the surface only by engraving (no applied glass) but with colored wings *beneath* the surface. This use of a double image is repeated over and over by Gallé (see 5, 7, 22, etc.). In addition, a third large ant lion-like creature (23f) is engraved on another side, its wings and yellow body embedded within the vessel wall.

An unusual feature of this object is the prominence of the interior (23d). Here the central insect appears as a glorious black silhouette hunting its prey – the winged yellow insects (23e), possibly mayflies, hidden from view by white "clouds" on the outside, clearly visible only from the *inside*. Also noteworthy is the Gallé signature (on the outside, 23g) with the "G" forming a stylized, winged insect.

23c)   Side right of 23a

23d) Inside of the coupe

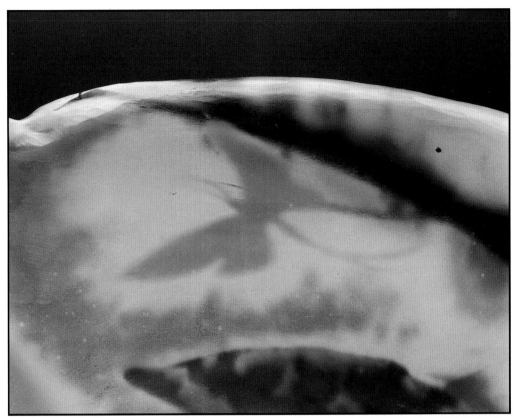

23e) Detail of inside

23f) Side right of 23c

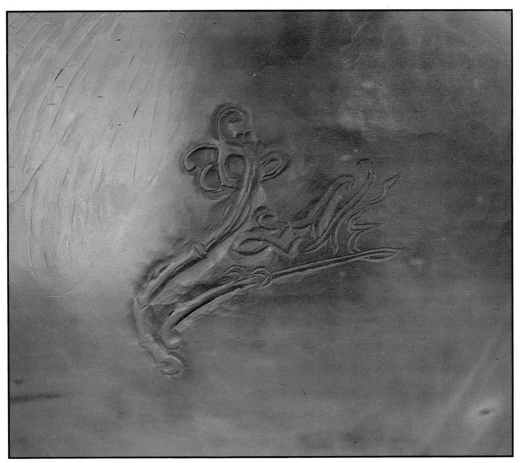

23g) **Detail showing signature**

Date: 1903 · H. 18.3 cm, D. 19.7 cm
Blown; marquetry and metallic foil inclusions; external marquetry and applied bits; patina-
tion; multilayered foot with applied bits; cut, engraved.
Signed: *Emile Gallé* on bowl
Collection: The Corning Museum of Glass (80.3.59) and private collection
Purchased by Edouard Hannon in 1903 for his house in Brussels

24a) **Dragonfly**

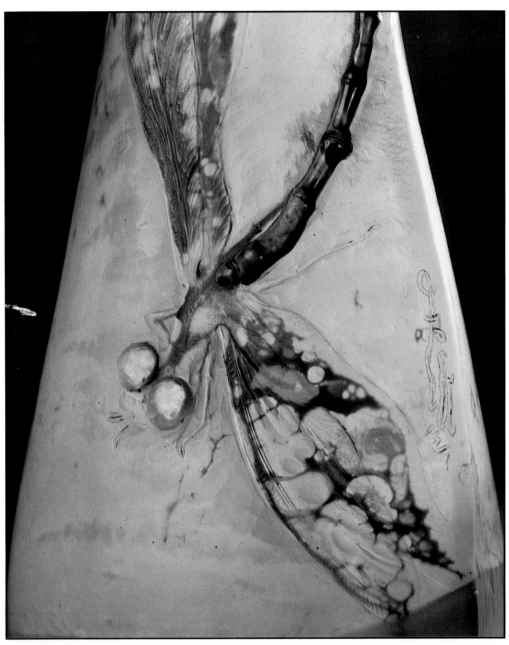

24b)   Detail of 24a

24) DRAGONFLY

A DRAGONFLY DIVES toward the water, its large predatory eyes glinting from yellow-gold and silver metal foil backings. In flight the legs of the dragonfly form a basket for catching insects. These engraved legs, all askew, add an element of contortion to the graceful curve of the body. The overall form of this vase is similar to the Iris (9).

One of the two techniques for which Gallé made patent applications in 1898 is prominent here: patina. Briefly, patina results from the decorative use of ashes from wood or coal combustion to create bubbles, sooty surface films, etc. – all considered as imperfections by most of the glass industry at that time. The mottled wings of the dragonfly and the ragged black form on the opposite side (24c) are examples. As discussed in relation to Blue Melancholia (38), Gallé at times uses his techniques in the abstract to generate interesting patterns, colors, textures, etc. – as with the back of this piece (24c). At other times he combines techniques to achieve realism, as with the dragonfly wings, where patina and engraving work together to create a recognizable image. Love of technique for its own sake and love of nature are never far apart in Gallé.

Date: About 1903-1904 · H. 29.1 cm; D. 16.2 cm
Signed (to right of dragonfly): *Gallé*
Blown; color casings at base; patina; metal foil; applied bits; cut, engraved
Collection: Philadelphia Museum of Art, Philadelphia, Pennsylvania
Acquired from the St. Louis Exposition (U.S.A.) of 1904

24c) Reverse side

25a) Beetle Vase

25b) Detail of 25a

25) BEETLE VASE

ONE ASPECT OF GALLÉ'S ASTONISHING VIRTUOSITY is that he can make us recognize images as both dreamlike symbols and living creatures. On this vase a beetle seems to devour slimy, decaying tropical fruit in the midst of murky leaves and twigs. Although the beetle is a male rhinoceros, among the largest of all insects, and a peaceful vegetarian, Gallé creates a menacing insect and makes the head, horns, and wing covers look as if they mirror the mysteries of the night sky—a fanciful interpretation.

Realistic details such as a patinated leaf over fat air bubbles show a spontaneity which reveals a love of material for its own sake. So Gallé moves from reality to dream.

Gallé uses still another member of the beetle family to illustrate the creative process of the symbolist artist:

> We do not know the name of the fine, thoughtful artist, the sculptor of Egypt, the royal goldsmith, magus, or decorator of temples who, having stopped to observe the carrying-on of a filthy little insect, the dung beetle, as it fashioned a ball of dung to deposit its eggs in the warmth of the Libyan sand, was moved by a kind of religious awe. He was the first to discover beyond all appearances the reflection of an august image: he invented the mystic jewel, the *sacred scarab*. The front legs of the insect—and later, in Phoenician imitations, its spread wings—support the solar globe, the origin of light and warmth; with its hind legs, it maternally rolls another celestial globe, the earth, in which it deposits the seeds of life. What remarkable testimony by the artist-inventor to the existence of a Divine Creator, to the providential bringing-together of planet and source of heat! Strange and ancient prescience of the planetary form of the earth itself, one might say: here is a symbol that is artistic, cosmographic, religious, and prophetic. (*Ecrits*, p. 214)

Dated: 1900 · H. 22.9 cm
Blown; overlays; patination; applied bits; engraved.
Signed: *Gallé 1900*
Collection: N. El Fituri, Geneva, Switzerland

The Beetle Vase resembles the "Forêt Javanaise" (number 5, plate 6, Exposition de l'Ecole de Nancy, Paris, 1903) and "La Forêt Guyanaise" (in the collection of the Musée de l'Ecole de Nancy).

25c) Reverse side

26a) Cicadas

26b) **Side right of 26a**

26, 27, 28) CICADAS

IN JAPAN, CICADAS are symbolic harbingers of death at the peak of happiness; in nature the grub spends years underground and has only a brief life (a few weeks) in the sunlight where it sings incessantly. Gallé seems to be mirroring the rigid posture of the cicada body in the bowl (26b), while in the bowl with metal foot (27, detail b) there appear to be two species, one with a greenish patination, the other with clear wings and black decorated body.

The vase (28) is probably the earliest in the group. On the basis of related ceramic pieces and drawings,* it may date from about 1881-1889 and in style seems to be a transition between the earlier enameled pieces and the later works with heavy applied decorations – the image of the cicada has been raised above the surrounding surface by mold blowing.

Number 26 reminds us of Gallé's preference for threatening edges (26c) as shown by the spiky pine needles in stark silhouette against the amber shading to white ground.

In the bowl with metal foot (27), the long thin leaves may belong to olive trees or be the seeds of an ash. Again, duality of images, things appearing in two ways, is apparent in the cicadas in flight (27b) where the lower one is reminiscent of an x-ray, while the upper is opaque and patinated.

(26)
Date: About 1900 · H. 19.7 cm; D. (max.) 18.1 cm; D. (base knop) 10 cm
Blown (probably in a mold); cased; cut and engraved
Signed (near single cicada resting on limb): *Gallé*
Collection: Private

26c)   Side left of 26a

27a) Cicadas

(27)
Date: About 1900 · H. 22.7 cm; D. (max.) 18.3 cm
Blown; cased; patina; cut and engraved. Metal base.
Signed: *Gallé*
Collection: Private

27b) Detail of 27a

28) Cicada

(28)
Date: About 1881-1889 · H. 33.3 cm; W. 14.3 cm
Mold-blown; internal coloring; enameled, gilt.
Signed: E (Cross of Lorraine) G (near base of Cicada) E. Gallé/Nancy/(Illegible)
(on base)
Collection: The Corning Museum of Glass, Corning, New York, No. 82.3.32

*"Meisenthal Oder Nancy? Addenda zu Emile Gallé," Brigitte Klesse, from Sonder-
druck aus dem Wallraf-Richartz-Jahrbuch. Band XLII, 1981. Köln: Dumont Buchverlag, pp. 176-177, illus. 15, 16.

29a) **Magnolia and Catkins**

29) MAGNOLIA AND CATKINS

ONE SIDE HAS a prominent flower, probably a magnolia in early spring; both sides show seed-bearing catkins, possibly of a weeping willow. A butterfly has landed on one catkin (29c).

Small details enhance this vase. A white blemish has become a tiny engraved butterfly (29c) resting on a bit of silvery foil embedded within the glass. On the same side, a strip of silvery metal foil descends from the rim and is connected to a strip of gold foil by surface engraving. Is this whole structure another catkin, one wonders? The catkins are a different colored glass from the surrounding surface – blonde against a turquoise-green ground. The base is a deep, muddy amber-brown into which some of the catkins descend, as if into water. The catkin on the left side makes this a dramatic descent, as it goes from blonde, engraved, rough surface (above) to flat, bright, patinated supernova (below).

The separation of color from light and dark values may seem impossible, but in reality it happens all the time. Think of a shiny strip of gold foil: the color is a constant, but it looks lighter or darker depending upon the angle of the light striking it. This separation is easy to accomplish in glass, and we see it frequently in Gallé.

29b) **Reverse side**

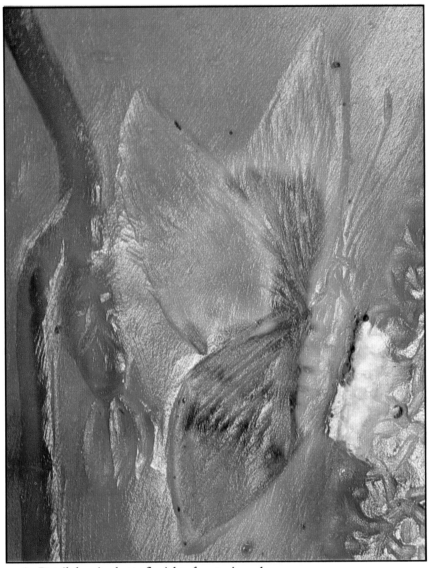

29c) Detail showing butterfly right of center in 29b

Color is inherent in the work itself – like the green wing tips of the butterfly (29c) or the gold foil strip laid under the catkin (29b, right center). Texturing by engraving gives a range of light and dark values to these colors as the angle of incident light changes. Freeing of color from the domination of light and shade nonetheless still holds color and texture in close juxtaposition. It is the utilization of glass to hold unlike elements together that so intrigues in this work.

Date: About 1895-1900 · H. 14.3 cm; W. (max.) 8.9 cm
Blown; internal striations; cased; marquetry; patina; foil inclusions; engraved
Signed (near red magnolia blossom): *Gallé*
Collection: Private

30a) Mushroom Lamp

30b) Detail of stems

30) MUSHROOM LAMP

EDISON INVENTED THE LIGHT BULB in 1879, and glassmakers, most notably Louis C. Tiffany in the United States, soon were designing lamps with glass shades to soften the harsh rays emitted by the new lights. This lamp is said to have been made as part of a dining room furnished like a forest, and at least four other versions, probably all made for the same interior, survive today.*

Philippe Garner praises this fascinating object in his biography of Gallé: "The mushroom is nowhere more potent or suggestive than in Gallé's disturbing masterpiece *Les Coprins*, whose three giant, overpowering mushrooms lay themselves open to numerous interpretations. There is an undeniably sexual quality to this sprouting cluster of Coprini but, above all, *Les Coprins* is surely to be seen as an allegory of the three ages of man, as a parable of the development of man's awareness, for, as the mushrooms burst forth, as they develop, so they become more sensuous, more enticing, until ultimately their form becomes dissipated."**

The mushrooms represented are probably inky caps in three stages of development. During spore ripening, the gills liquefy (autodigestion), the edges of the caps become ragged, and the mushrooms begin to look more and more like open umbrellas. Healthy inky caps are edible, but Gallé's version should not be used as a field guide illustration. The stems are stylized with prominent ridges created by blowing into a ribbed mold. Notice that the tallest is green, perhaps denoting maturity, in contrast to the blue, younger stems. Flecks of metal foil are suspended in the interior of each stem. The caps are covered with oval wheel cuts, either vertical or horizontal, and in the case of the medium-sized cap, some lines are etched. These indicate patterns found on real mushrooms – but could they also be meant to evoke dew?

Details of cutting and patination are not subliminal as we have seen in many of Gallé's smaller works, but in scale they seem appropriate to an object meant to compete for attention in a large room. In its undulating surfaces, voluptuous overtones, and "larger-than-life" size, the work is like soft, surreal sculptures by Claes Oldenburg from the 1960s and seventies. Both artists humanize the products of technology; Gallé does so with organic forms.

Date: About 1902 · H. (overall) 83.8 cm, D. (base) 31.4 cm
Blown; cased; internal patination; cut, etched; wrought iron base and mounts;
electric light fittings.
Collection: Johanna Walker, England

*See Bloch-Dermant, p. 90 and Garner, p. 31. Other examples of the lamp are in the collections of the Musée de l'Ecole de Nancy and the Kitazawa Museum of Art in Japan, and in private collections in New York and Europe. A catalog for the *Exposition de l'Ecole de Nancy à Strasbourg*, 1908, lists this design and names the following "collaborators": Louis Hestaux, Paul Nicolas, Paul Holderbach.

**Garner, *Emile Gallé*, pp. 139-141.

30c) Side view

31a) Butterflies

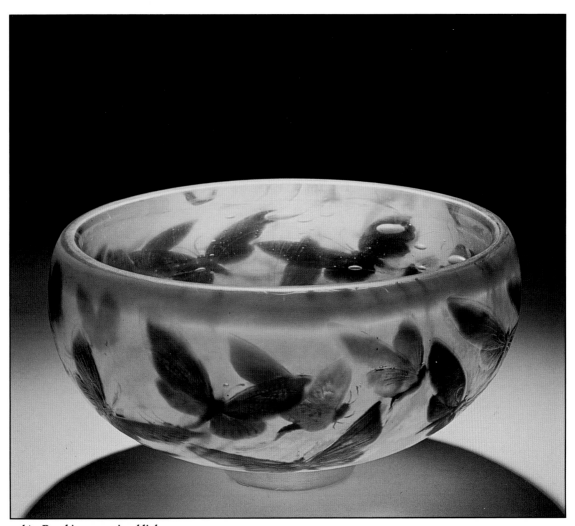

31b) Bowl in transmitted light

31) BUTTERFLIES

BUTTERFLIES APPEAR TO ENCIRCLE THE BOWL above water, indicated by the bubbly, striated glass. We know these are butterflies rather than mayflies or other winged insects because Gallé shows them here with clubbed antennae and discal cells (visible in 31a: discal cells are diamond-shaped areas engraved at the wing base).

This piece represents the epitome of Gallé's naturalism. His insects are so real that they become living creatures entrapped in glass. But once again (36 and 11) the bowl must be handled to be fully appreciated. The butterflies exist both as color (amber *inside* the glass) and as engraving (on the white casing of the bowl's surface). When color and engraving interact, the insects appear bluish because of the white over the amber. Handling also increases our appreciation of the bowl's realism, for while the eye and the camera see the internal insects as fuzzy forms never quite in focus, the mind, in combining the multiple viewpoints after repeated handlings, compensates for the distortion of the glass, and we remember the butterflies as vividly real and precisely detailed.

Date: About 1890-1900
H. 8 cm; D. (max.) 15.7 cm; D. (base pad) 4.6 cm
Blown; cased; internal marquetry; engraved.
Signed (above base): *Gallé*
Collection: Private

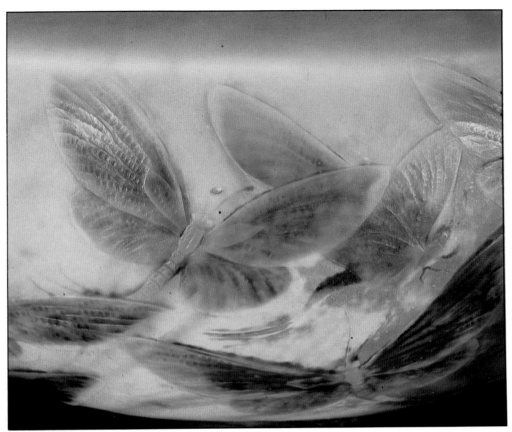

31c) Detail of center

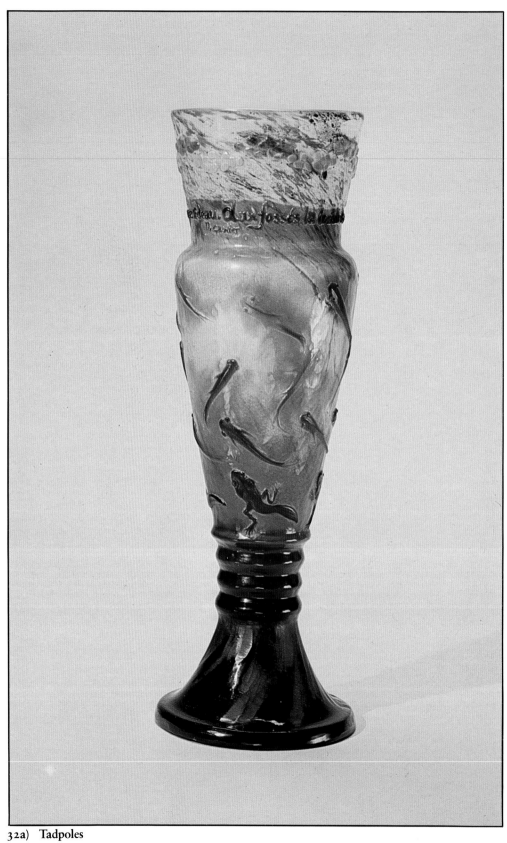

32a) Tadpoles

32) TADPOLES

Upon the moats, the duckweed
With its leaves of verdigris
Extends a curtain of sea-green.
(inscription on the vase)
    From Théophile Gautier
      "The Castle of Memory," in *Enamels and Cameos*

TADPOLES BECOME FROGS before our very eyes, as minnows swim in the muddy water, and duckweed (*Lemna minor*) floats on the surface. The life cycle of the plant, whose colors (32c) go from green (young and healthy) to yellow and pink (old and dying), is represented. The streamers which trail from the plants are roots; the bottom of the vase, with its rings, may represent layers of mud. The subject here, apparently, is metamorphosis (tadpole to frog), reminding us that Gallé appreciates time's passage, exhibiting nature in slow transition (witness also Orchids, 19 and 20 and the Barley vase, 14).

The notion of duality (as in 7, 23) is also illustrated here with some minnows in raised relief and some that disappear into the hot amber (muddy?) background (32b) to produce ghostly images. The piece also exhibits the inconsistency we often associate with Gallé (The Pasteur Coupe, 4, is a prime example). The treatment of the tadpoles is realistic, but the representation of the duckweed is not. Here the leaves are stylized clusters of ovals like tiny oil storage tanks (32c) floating half submerged on their sides, attached by engraved threads (roots) of glass reaching into the muddy water containing the tadpoles.

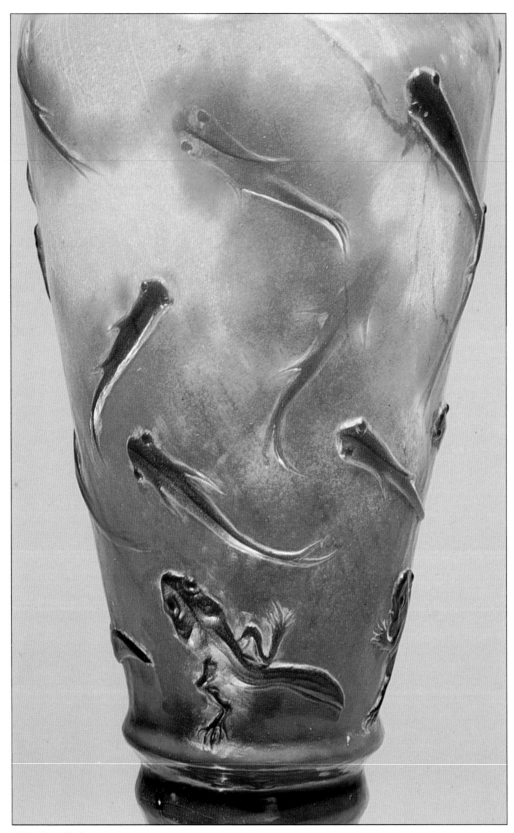

32b) Detail of center

32c) **Detail of top**

Date: About 1889-1900 (new edition of the 1889 version)
H. 31.4 cm, D. (max.) 10.6 cm
Blown (probably mold-blown); cased, inclusions; cut and engraved
Signed (above rings at base): *Gallé*
Inscribed (below rim): *Aux fossés la*
         *lentille d'deau, De ses feuilles**
         vert-de-/grisées étale le glaque rideau
         Th. Gautier
Collection: Musée de l'Ecole de Nancy, Nancy, France

* Gallé substituted the word *feuilles* (leaves) for the original *taches* (spots) in this
poem. The substitution is reasonable for a plant lover.

33a) Sea Lily

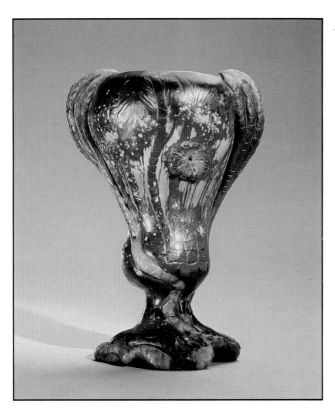

33) SEA LILY

Curious anomaly! fantastic element! in which the animal
kingdom blossoms and the vegetable does not.
        Jules Verne, *20,000 Leagues under the Sea*

THE OVERALL FORM is that of the top of a sea lily (crinoid). Applied to one side (33a) is a complete version of the creature, while the opposite side (33b) has an applied button-like disk – a component of the sea lily stem, possibly a fossil. For a long time these creatures were known only from fossil remains, but the first live deep sea specimens were discovered during the later part of the nineteenth century. It is uncertain whether Gallé knew of this discovery.

Like the *Sea Horses* (34), this piece has a visceral look, as if it (like our own internal organs) does not thrive in daylight. There is something eerie in Gallé's infatuation with deep sea creatures (see especially the notes on the Hand, 39), and this vase is doubly eerie: a deep-water theme, perhaps a long-buried fossil. But of course these ideas are also the logical result of Gallé's naturalism: "Science, in short, has opened new horizons for the decorative artist." (Emile Gallé, *Ecrits*, p. 224).

Date: About 1895-1904 · H. 14 cm; W. (max.) 10.3 cm
Blown; cased; applied bits; cut and engraved · Signed (on side): *Gallé*
Collection: Private

34a) Sea Horses

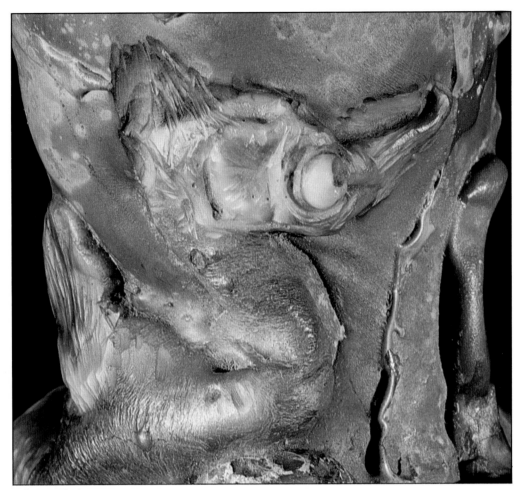

34b) Detail of 34a

34, 35) SEA HORSES, SEA DRAGON

Captain Nemo himself could have explored these pieces (and others such as the Deep Sea vase, 36). They are reminders of Gallé's interest in oceanography as a source for new works:

These secrets of the Ocean are brought forth to us by brave deep-sea divers. They empty their marine harvest which passes from the laboratory to the studios of decorative art and to the museums of models. They draw and publish these undreamt-of materials for the artist: enamels and cameos from the sea.

(Emile Gallé, *Ecrits*, p. 225)

35a) Sea Dragon

35b) Side left of 35a

Sea Horses (34) is one of Gallé's invented forms (like the pine vases, 21 and 22, and the Rhubarb Coupe, 17). While the spiraled handle and shape evoke more classical vessels, the overall impression is of a fossilized sea fragment. The uppermost sea horse is a male – notice its pouch for holding eggs. It is a study in textures: shiny, red sponge or kelp-like branches rise from the base; the body of the upper sea horse resembles faceted jasper while the lower one has a texture like wrinkled elephant skin; the rocks or sponge at the base are pitted like cinders. Amid all this, nothing is fully realized, finely executed, or finally finished; everything is compromised in favor of the accidental. Everything meets its opposite. What should continue (the kelp) is stopped; what begins straight becomes twisted (the upper sea horse). The shape is neither the support nor the supported but part of each; the texture of the background is smooth and hard, wrinkled and soft. There are those who feel one of the hallmarks of genius is unpredictability – try to guess what Mozart's next note will be – and so Gallé always surprises with these strange combinations (as in the huge butterflies and fussy little cupid in 2, the oyster-blue sheen on the hot amber palm of the Hand, 39). Are they the result of intentions that went astray, or happily seized accidents? In 35, a creature resembling a leafy sea dragon (common to Australia) rises from an ocean of what is probably algae. On the base (35d) is a sea star. The twisted, irregular shape especially noticeable just above the base is formed by cutting, and there are pleasing interplays of thicknesses: the applied ivory-like

sea creature (one can see its thickness in 35b); the raised amber seaweed, the result of engraving, overlaying purple seaweed and yellow forms *within* the glass (35c). Again, we have a study in textures like Sea Horses (34) but more harmonious, less visceral, the internal colors having "...the freshness of shades of watercolors, but a simple and recent watercolor that has not yet dried on the paper...."

Emile Gallé (*Ecrits*, p. 175)

(34) SEA HORSES
Dated: 1901 · H. 19 cm
Blown; internal colors; applied bits; patina; engraved.
Signed (on base): *Joseph Reinach/Emile Gallé/1901* and inscribed on one side: *Vitam impendere Vero (Life depends on Truth)*
Collection: Musée des Arts Décoratifs, Paris, France
Note: Reinach, contemporary of Gallé, was a writer, politician, secretary of the Dreyfusards, and published a chronicle of the affair in several volumes.

(35) SEA DRAGON
Date: About 1900-1904 · H. (approx.) 30 cm, D. (base) 10.1 cm
Blown; internal colors; cased; applied bits; cut and engraved
Signed (above base): *Gallé*
Collection: Private

36a) Deep Sea

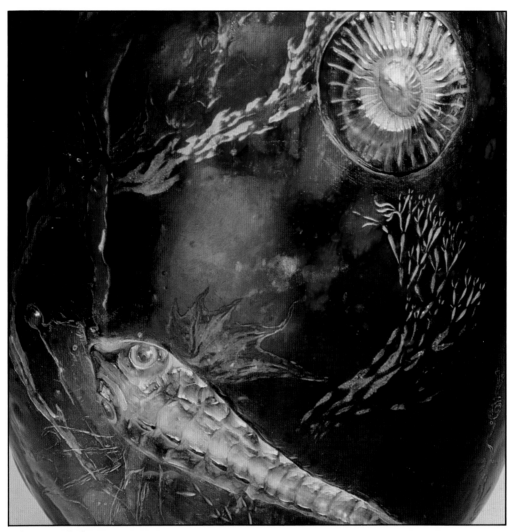

36b) Detail of 36a

36, 37) DEEP SEA, DEEP SEA (1889)

Flotsam

"GLASS BOTTLE, flattened bottle; edges as though worn down, lustered and polished, polished by being continually thrown up against the beach. Missive emptied of its message, filled with mystery, swollen with shadow and silence. Only the marine grass now inscribes itself within, green and bubbly calligraphy, dried with silver sand. An algae disjoints bleeding bodies. The jellyfish which is stuck to it makes the blue phosphorus of its gelatins glow in the deep redness, fruit-flower and eye which lies in wait and which eats. . . .

The other side of the glass tells how, rocked on the warm oils of the tropics, it drank the color of the rays which dye the islands with blood, and checker all the feathers and all the flowers there with red, orange, and indigo.

Mounet-Sully had come to see glass worked. With his head bent, he was contemplating the *Flotsam* placed on his knees, and rolling it between his feverish fingers. The surrounding house and countryside were awaiting something very beautiful which was about to be declaimed. Slowly, very low, he began to recite the poem:

> *Oh! how many sailors, how many captains*
> *Who have joyously left for distant courses…*

When the poet, when the artist had done, no one dared to trouble with a thanks the broad expanse created. Breath fled through the windows and the too narrow frame of the place. But Hernani with his eyes and his palms continued to caress the *Flotsam*." Emile Gallé (*Ecrits*, pp. 161-162).

Although it is uncertain that "Flotsam" refers directly to the Deep Sea Vase, it is an apt description. The ribbed, disk-shaped form applied near the upper right shoulder is probably a jellyfish; silver foil under the appliqués flashes blue; the surfaces are deep red and appear worn down. The winged creature applied near the bottom is probably a bottom-dwelling fish, perhaps an armored poacher. The way the sea plants are treated indicates that at least three different kinds of algae or sponge are represented.

The texture of this piece is very rich, with a variety of surfaces as much to be felt as seen (See also 18). Fat bubbles on the side are easy to touch, hard to see; the yellow plant life layered within is easy to see, impossible to touch. This again points up one of Gallé's basic ideas—to bridge the gulf between the natural and man-made, to establish an appealing interaction between the inherent look of glass—its transparency, its impurities or patinas—and what the glass represents: in this case, ocean life. For example, his sea is red, and red is a wonderful, challenging color for the glassmaker (witness medieval windows, the ruby red panes of which were highly prized), beautiful in itself but red also because of the brillance it gives to the silver of the fish, to the yellow of the plants, to the very concept of sun-drenched tropical water and the blood of the sailors it consumed. Engraving can dramatically modify surfaces; a similar vase (37), not engraved, has a less finished, fresh-from-the-furnace look.

(36) DEEP SEA
Date: About 1889-1903 · H. 21.4 cm, W. (max.) 14.3 cm, D. (rim) 7.6 cm
Blown; cased; metal foil and applied bits; engraved
Signed (to right of fish form);
Collection: Musée de l'Ecole de Nancy, Nancy, France

(37) DEEP SEA (1889)
Dated: 1889 · H. 21.3 cm
Blown; cased; metal foil and applied bits ; acid-etched inscriptions
Signed: *E* (Cross of Lorraine) *G*; *Emile Gallé a´ Nancy* with *E* (Cross of Lorraine) *G*; *Exposition/1889.*
Inscribed (on back): *Roisseau mauve(?),/ porte à l'ocean multicolore/ le defi de nos rives,/ la plume émaillée/ du martin pêcheur (The mauve stream/ carries to the multicolored ocean/ the challenge of our shores,/ the enameled plume/ of a kingfisher)*
Collection: Kunstmuseum Düsseldorf

37) Unfinished 1889

38a) Blue Melancholy

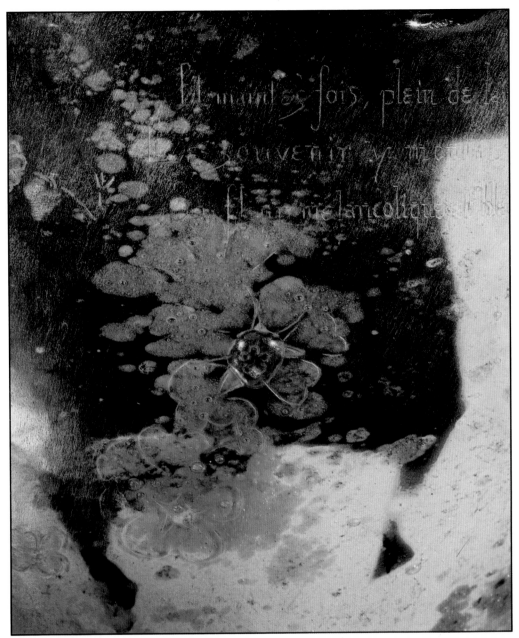

38b) Detail of 38a

38) BLUE MELANCHOLY

*How many times a languid
Memory shows the heart
Its blue and melancholy flower*

(inscription on the bowl)

Rollinat

38c) Reverse side

FIVE-PETALED FLOWERS ENGRAVED over cloudy patches of blue are probably forget-me-nots; the shell engraved on the base and the muddy patina evoke the environment around a pond or stream.

The overall composition of the piece shows a graceful interplay of modest parts where chance has been allowed to play a role. It is not uncommon for bubbles or blisters to become decorative elements, and here we see a tiny engraved flower centered on a bubble which itself forms the center of a larger flower (38b). The final position and color variations of the muddy patina, red ground, and clouds of blue could not have been predetermined or altered after the piece cooled, but what could be anticipated is that interesting edges and shifts of color would occur. The blood red ground (reminiscent of Deep Sea, 36) became an unexpected contrasting color (unexpected in the context of ponds): notice how light, transmitted *through* the wall of the bowl, gives the red a bright value which accentuates the central blue flowers (38a). The large, teardrop-shaped bubble (38d), precariously close to the surface, is a subtle variation best experienced by touching it.

Various surface abrasions tighten the composition. The misty blue patches are

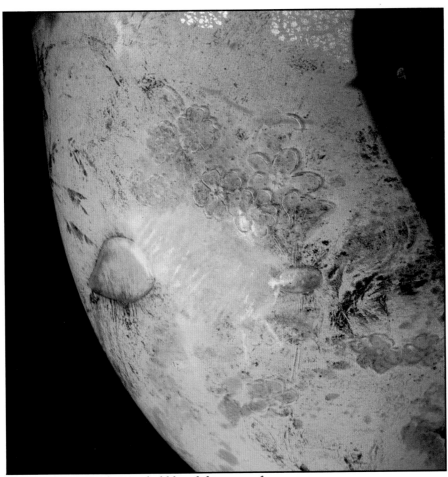

38d) Detail of 38c showing bubble at left, matt surface at center

engraved, which serves to contain the blue, intensify its edges, and identify the flowers. The matt surface (probably acid-etched) imparts a very subtle effect. Between the bubble and patch of flowers (38d) it forms a haze over part of the blue area. Such details point up the indistinct boundary between technical effects used to *represent* (engraved flowers) and technical effects used for their *own sake* (as colors, form, texture).

Date: 1892 · H. 13.3. cm, D. (rim)13.6
Blown; cased; internal patina; color decoration; foil inclusions; cut, engraved, probably acid-etched
Signed (base): *Emile Gallé/Nancy/1892*
Inscribed (below rim): *Et maintes fois, plein de langeur,*
                  Le souvenir y montre au coeur
                  Sa fleur mélancholique et bleue
                            Rollinat
Collection: The Chrysler Museum, Norfolk, Virginia, The Jean Outland Chrysler Collection in tribute to Lida and Grover Outland GEFG 66.4

39a) Palm in transmitted light

39b)   Palm in reflected light

39) HAND

Man — a free man — always loves the sea
And in its endlessly unrolling surge
Will contemplate his soul as in a glass
. . .
— who has sounded to its depths the human heart?
And who has plucked its riches from the sea? —
So jealously they guard their secrets both!*
                    Emile Gallé (*Ecrits*, pp. 224-225)

*Baudelaire; Trans. Richard Howard

39c) Back of hand in transmitted light

A HAND covered in seaweed rises from the ocean depths. This is the only work in the group that seems to have no functional purpose – it might "contain," but only a little; it might hold finger rings, but only one or two. In fact, even the organic – Pines (21), Rhubarb Coupe (17) – have formal elements supporting them or rhythmically establishing base and rim. How satisfactory is the Hand as sculpture? As decoration? Why is it so alone in this galaxy of great pieces? It seems as if the Hand is a final statement on Gallé's attitude toward form, texture, technique, and subject – final in that it is enough, but does it succeed as sculpture and so carry him to new heights? Somehow it remains decoration, superb, among his best, but still a fragment. Why? Perhaps because the *means* of its accomplishment and the *ideas* it embodies are the sum of Gallé's vision – not the final object itself, not the end result.

In a sculpture, form and decoration are inseparable, and the artist's vision is made manifest in the totality of the work. But Gallé thinks of a hand emerging from water, covered with seaweed, shells, whatever; he sees the hot glass – dichroic, veined, cased, being manipulated into shape, with ribbons and strings and bits of hot glass added this way and that; the surface is pushed and paddled, fumed and abraded – a wondrous mix of texture and transparency, color shifts, intertwinings, bubbles, pools, and spots. But it is not a very convincing hand, not a very specific hand – it is a decoration, not a sculpture.

Date: About 1900 · H. 32.5 cm, W. (max) 13.2 cm
Hot worked glass; applied bits; patination; some surface abrasion.
Signed (near base of wrist): *Gallé*
Collection: Musée de l'Ecole de Nancy, Nancy, France

40) BOTTOM OF THE SEA

SHARING SPACE WITH SOME OF GALLÉ'S most distinguished creations in glass, the display vitrine (Bottom of the Sea) is the only piece of furniture included in this exhibition. It is most fitting that this extraordinary piece, lost to memory save for a single known contemporary illustration and now on public view for the first time in many decades, should be included in an exhibition of Gallé's achievements in glass. Within its wooden structure it exploits the medium of glass in a most imaginative way and perhaps can be described as Gallé's most successful experiment in combining the two media.

A study of the cabinet gives substance and detail to its image as reproduced in *La Lorraine Artiste et Littéraire* with an obituary of Gallé published in January 1905. Raised on four bowed legs, each carved with an octopus, and, indeed, spread like open tentacles, the vitrine is glazed on all four sides and top with deeply bowed side windows. On the narrower sides are two shelves of colorless glass internally flecked with green and red, evoking the image of algae in water. Sea creatures carved in colored glass and shell are applied to the sculpted wood framework. Gallé had used similar applications in full relief on glass vases with aquatic themes. Here, glass combines with wood to describe and symbolize the hidden depths of the oceans.

The vitrine is remarkable on several counts. Its visual lightness and elegance distinguish it from so much of Gallé's furniture, all too often characterized by fascinating details within ponderous and ungainly forms. Gallé's interest in furniture design dated to 1885, and his first major exhibition was in 1889. His style was based on principles of naturalism which he defined in the essay "Le Mobilier Contemporain orné d'après la Nature," published in November/December 1900 in the *Revue des Arts Décoratifs*. Much of his furniture, however, shows a strong historicism and a lack of invention in the forms, despite the lush and richly symbolist naturalism in the details of carved structural elements and of marquetry paneling. This vitrine is a notable exception.

It is also remarkable in its unusual combination of media. Bronze details such as hinges, decorative lock-plates, and handles are commonplace in Gallé's furniture. Glass details are rare. The few examples include, perhaps most notably, the carved glass incorporated in the bed, *Aube et Crépuscule,* and the bulging colored glass dragonfly eyes of the vitrine for M. Hirsch, both pieces dating from 1904.

It is significant that this interest in mixing media should correspond to the final phase of Gallé's furniture design, perhaps representing the culmination of his achievement in this field—the synthesis of the two media in which his talents had reached their most distinguished expression.

Bottom of the Sea is surely most remarkable as a rare example of Gallé's furniture to have as its theme the mysterious depths of the sea. This theme had inspired numerous creations in glass and is one of the most interesting facets of Gallé's symbolist repertoire. It is tempting to quote Baudelaire as a source of inspiration in this context, for he evidently inspired Gallé in other specific pieces such as the cabinet *Les Fleurs du Mal* of 1896 and the desk *La Forêt Lorraine* of 1900. Like them, this vitrine is richly symbolist, and just as they call forth exotic flora and lush forest, Bottom of the Sea brings to mind the murky but magical depths of mystery evoked by Baudelaire in the poem "L'Homme et la Mer" quoted with the Hand, 39, above.

PHILIPPE GARNER

Date: About 1904 · H. 137.2 cm, Width 119.9 cm x 66 cm
Wood, probably ebony; glass, shell, and possibly amber inlays; glass shelves and cover glass; copper alloy handles
Collection: Private

COMMENTARY

IS THE GLASS OF EMILE GALLÉ *still* ugly? Does that tendril-like signature of his still evoke only recollections of acid-etched cameos in browns and ambers? Does the purity of our taste still prefer its forms unadorned? The purpose of this exhibition — and catalog — is to make us all take another look, to put aside our prejudices and reconsider.

In these few dozen pieces, chosen from the very best of his work, we see a glassmaker who is at once an artist and a poet, a scientist and a technician, a craftsman, an inventor, and a manufacturer. His objects combine decorative techniques — inclusions, enameling, marquetry, engraving, staining, abrading and on and on — with an opulence that seems almost too exotic to bear. Quite at the other end of the spectrum from the lab flask martini pitcher, his work stands among the very richest and most elaborate in the whole history of glassmaking.

But there is more. As an artist who uses glass to give his symbols tangible reality, does he not presage the whole studio movement? At the end of the 19th century the imitation of historic styles of decoration was the preoccupation of most great glassmakers. Technique was triumphant. In these pieces technique is in the service of Gallé's ideas; no matter how innovative or elaborate, it always serves, it never dominates.

To put it another way, he carries craft into art by subjugating mastery of the glassmaking medium to the feelings he has for his subjects — nature, myth, man. The pieces in this exhibition are not decorated objects; they are the embodiments of attitudes. Is that not what contemporary artists working in glass also strive for?

Gallé, however, is more than a historical precedent; he is so inventive — discovering and patenting all sorts of coloring agents, corrosive systems, forming devices; so concerned with justice, with nature, and with truth that he alludes through symbol as well as the inscribed word to some of the most powerful thought of his time — including his own; so humane and inspiring in his relations with the people who worked for him (300 of them!) that the hallmark of personal creativity — spontaneity — is everywhere evident. Add to all this the distinction of his presence in the great expositions of the day plus his role as civic leader and patriot and we have in Gallé a truly inspiring model for those who would make art of glass.

Precursor of the 20th-century glass artist, Gallé may also be a herald of the future. In denying the transcendence of form over decoration (let alone function over form), does he not anticipate the latest emerging attitudes? In his quest for preciousness, for richness, for opulence, is he not aligned to the newest trends? Most importantly in his passion for nature — derived from a profound knowledge of botany — is he not combining the ecologist's determination to preserve with a Proustian dedication to remember — while simultaneously leading us all back or forward to the Ruskinian notion that "You never will love art well, till you love what she mirrors better"?

THOMAS S. BUECHNER

FOOTNOTES

1. Arnold Hauser, *The Social History of Art,* Volume 2, New York: Vintage Books, 1951, p. 65.

2. George D. Painter, *Marcel Proust: A Biography,* Volume 1, New York: Vintage Books, 1978, p. 227.

3. Stuart H. Hughes, *Consciousness and Society,* New York: Vintage Books, 1977, p. 41.

4. Jules Henrivaux, quoted in Janine Bloch-Dermant, *The Art of French Glass 1860-1914,* New York: The Vendome Press, 1980, p. 132.

5. Charles de Meixmoron de Dombasle, "Résponse du Président M. Ch. de Meixmoron de Dombasle au Récipiendaire M. Emile Gallé. Académie de Stanislas, Séance solanelle 17.5.1900." Mémoires de l'Académie de Stanislas, Nancy 1899/1900, pp. 1-25. Readers are reminded that the earliest biographies of Gallé are not free from error; Charpentier discusses some of these in "Remarques sur les premieres biographies de Gallé parues de son temps."

6. Bloch-Dermant, p. 54.

7. Ada Polak, *Modern Glass,* London: Faber and Faber, 1962, p. 20.

8. Meixmoron, pp. L-LII.

9. Victor Arwas, *Glass: Art Nouveau to Art Deco,* New York: Rizzoli, 1977, p. 84.

10. Philippe Garner, *Emile Gallé,* New York: Rizzoli, 1979, pp. 118-120.

11. Garner, p. 59.

12. Bloch-Dermant, p. 132.

13. Gerald Reitlinger, *The Economics of Taste,* Volume Three. The Art Market in the 1960s, London: Barrie and Jenkins, 1970, p. 537.

14. Polak, p. 20.

15. Technical information about Gallé's working process is available in the Exposition Notices in *Ecrits pour l'Art* (see bibliography); an English translation is available in the Library of The Corning Museum of Glass. The Library also has correspondence, drawings and working instructions by Gallé and his associates. Patent requests made by Gallé pertaining to patina and marquetry processes are published in English by Bloch-Dermant pp. 121-125. The section on glass from the 1889 Exposition notice is reprinted at the end of this catalog.

16. Bloch-Dermant, p. 98 and Garner, p. 95.

17. Jules Henrivaux, *La Verrerie au XXe siècle,* Paris, 1903, p. 583.

18. John Rewald, *The History of Impressionism,* New York: The Museum of Modern Art, 1973, p. 426.

19. Bloch-Dermant, p. 55.

GALLÉ'S NOTES ON GLASS PRODUCTION

Emile Gallé submitted the following notes to the Jury of the Paris Universal Exposition of 1889. They were later reprinted in his *Ecrits pour l'art: floriculture, art décoratif, notices de'exposition 1884-1889*. Ed. Henriette Gallé-Grim. Paris: Librairie Renouard, 1908. [Reprint: Marseille: Laffitte Reprints, 1980.]

Notes on the Production of Deluxe Glass and Crystal Ware
by
EMILE GALLÉ

Members of the Jury

Since the Universal Exhibition of Paris in 1878, I have entered no international competitions. Permit me, therefore, to retrace the development of the various branches of my glass production since the last time you were able to examine it.

Limiting myself to the specialty of deluxe crystal manufacture I isolated the following problems as the object of my research.

1) New effects of craftsmanship. Compositions designed to give vitreous matter new, unexpected, and precious aspects. The search for coloration and decoration in the mass.

2) To extend the techniques for enriching glass through vitrifiable colors and enamels. New enamels.

3) To complement the tools of the crystal engraver; the development and application of the resources available through different means of engraving crystal and glass: intaglio, relief, acid, diamond-point. Exquisite execution and works of art.

4) Practical applications for industry. The contributions made to glass production by aesthetic judgment.

5) To create a special studio for decorative composition specifically related to the refinement of crystal and glass. To introduce French crystal and the modern style into collections of art objects and curiosity pieces.

In the hasty elaboration of these propositions, I hearby offer you, Gentlemen, several examples from among the three hundred pieces of crystal in Class 19 that represent my latest production.

Techniques

New Colorations

In 1878 I submitted for your consideration a potassium-based glass colored with a slight amount of cobalt oxide that produced a rather pleasant sapphire tone. The decorative uses to which I put this glass created something of a vogue for that shade of color. I marketed it commercially under the name "clair-de-lune" and it was reproduced successively in France, in England (under the name "Moonlight-glass") and in Germany (under the name "Mondschein"). Since that time there is hardly a factory that has not manufactured the "clair-de-lune"; it has now entered into the public domain. Following my submissions to the *Union centrale* of decorative arts in 1884, the same thing happened. Contemporary manufacturers did not hestitate to imitate in the manner of my own production the yellowish tones of blonde oyster shells, misted over with red and bluish hues. I had produced these effects by projecting onto marble pounded opal and red glass with copper protoxide, gathered by the glassmaker around a hot gob. These first experiments were still rather primitive; their success, nonetheless, was considerable at the time. They have, however, been entirely surpassed by the many techniques I have perfected and present to you today.

Since 1878 I have produced a certain number of colors that are more or less smoky and blackish, smudged and greenish, resulting either from iron protoxide or chromium oxide, or on other occasions from various combinations of iron, cobalt, and manganese oxides. I have also produced a potassium-based, vaguely two-toned glass with a pale leek-green hue and another green coloration also marked by some dichroism, with a sodium base, etc....

This year I am presenting a large number of colors that are new or rare in the making of glass goblets, two of which – and this is the obvious reason for their rarity – are the result of materials whose price is prohibitive from the perspective of industrial production: iridium and thallium. Within this collection, some yellows, browns, and iridescent greens are derived from silver and sulphur; a peacock-blue is derived from copper and iron and some browns derive from sulphur and catechu. Other colorations are not solid but complicated by varied tones that are incorporated into the mass; these came about as a result of my desire to reproduce natural materials – hard stones and gems and the precious accidents that are contained within quartz, agates, ambers, and jades.

Hence the jasper-like formations and the many marbled compositions, some opaque, others transparent; the "kneaded" mixtures, the hot applications, the superimposition of variously colored layers and the interpellation of decorative effects, if I may put it thus, between two layers of glass – effects that are at once stable yet left to chance. The articulation of these unique pieces is controlled by myself personally during the glassmaker's work, from the preparation of the compositions that are designed to marble and vein right through to their arrangement – whether accidental or perfectly controlled and planned in advance. The arborizations, the designs in the form of seaweed, butterflies, birds, and metallic leaves, fall into this category.

For the production of these polychromatic pieces, I was obliged to adapt no fewer than a hundred preparations and compositions, and this after much experimentation. Their combinations have, however, allowed me to achieve an infinite variety of accidents and nuances that are absolutely novel in the art of glassmaking.

I would also like to draw your attention, Gentlemen, to the colored bubbles and luster that were achieved through the projection of materials that, on contact with melting crystal, emit gases that create a mass of bubbles within the vitreous flux; these reduce to iridescences that line the bubbles with a thin metallic deposit.

I have also succeeded in obtaining superficial colorations, tints, reflections, singeings, and metallizations or deoxidations in which the metallic oxide of the composition is reduced to solid, brilliant, little drops that emboss the mass that contains them. These flickers of light, these metallic pearls and iridescences are a product of the reductive or oxidizing effect of the kiln's atmosphere on the gobs that are introduced into the glory hole; while still hot they were covered with special compositions. I would like to point out the beautiful lustrous effects that are derived from the reheating of glass with copper protoxide. In this instance, an element of chance decisively enters into play; it seems impossible to regulate this process so as to obtain any two pieces that are more or less identical.

Any summary of my research would necessarily be of only modest interest, Gentlemen, were it not for the applied uses to which I have put this knowledge. Here therefore are several examples of that work as exhibited in Class 19 and in the vestibule of honor.

Imitations of Hard Stones. Crystals Resembling Smoky Quartz and Amethyst Quartz.
It is well known that manganese oxide colors vitreous matter in rich or dull shades of violet depending on whether it is of a sodium or potassium base. Quartz, however, is rarely of a solid, unified color; rather, it is streaked or cloudy. The procedures that I have described above allowed me to reproduce those accidents of nature that divide beams of light in a manner pleasing to the eye and break the monotony of tone with local nuances. You will find among my entries pieces in which the purplish coloration is effected with marblings, jasper-like or agate-like formations and cloudings; elsewhere the color is condensed in places. Compositions No. 121 and 92, made with manganese peroxide maintained at its maximum oxidation, offer a trout-colored, speckled effect while numbers 81 and 82 resemble seaweed.

I have been able to reproduce dazzling cracks in certain quartzes by throwing cold water on the vase during the glasswork; this is a well-known technique. These very thick pieces are indeed well disposed to the dousing which then provokes the break into cracks. On occasion I have also used threads of amianthus and micaceous grains as in the following examples. No. 3: a vase of uneven thickness, stained with a manganese preparation, with Vercingetorix as its subject, engraved and gilded. No. 301: a Medici vase, amethyst glass, with a cloudy agate effect produced by the incorporation of a semi-opaque glass called alabaster or rice-paste which takes the form of a discordant porphyrized composition within the mass or produces a fine crackling. A similar composition is to be found in No. 98, a fountain basin which the *Journal of Saint-Petersburg* described in lyrical terms; it is made with manganese and a layer of ruby crystal and then is marbled with various preparations composed principally of gold and silver.

The juxtaposition or welding of bands of purplish crystal – more or less blue or red – and of opaque black paste to form a single vase provided a surprising and rich result. I then completed this work by etching the black layers.

In Item No. 16 the white base and neck of the vase have a black coating with moths chiseled in relief; they (the base and neck) are separated by an amethyst ball, and the entire thing takes the shape of a horn. Similarly, in item No. 127, the purplish-blue gob has a level edge that is welded to that of another white gob which is in turn overlaid with an opaque black paste; as the two compositions are not unharmonious, we were able to make of them a single undivided bowl that is richly engraved. A bowl engraved with fine black cameos is supported by a tender-hued amethyst foot on which I have engraved the following inscription: "Sweet amethyst consoles the blackest sorrows."

As a final example of this type I present the flask that was offered to the President of the Republic by the distillers' collective: On two layers of rusty black and crimson-shaded violet are etched the fruits and flowering branches of the *Illicium anisatum* (the star anise) with this motto: "Through sweetness shall I conquer."

Black (hyalith)
This composition could appear rather sad; but the etching brings to light clouded, greenish hues that the engraver can manipulate successfully, as in item No. 122. The black coating of this long-necked goblet has been carved with mists and dragonfly wings. Similarly a small vase has been finely etched with a *Cupid Chasing Black Butterflies*. I think I can attribute the gray glint that renders this material so iridescent to the contact during production with the carbon deposits of the glory hole that provoked an incipient reduction of the iron peroxide.

Imitations of Amber
I have assembled several pieces among my entries to the Exhibition of 1889 in which I have used the ancient techniques for manufacturing yellow; to them I have added new effects in direct imitation of pieces of red or gray amber. For example, No. 290, a vase decorated with cherries in a cameo; No. 300, a basin that resembles crude amber, flecked with little particles in its mass; No. 141, olive-yellow glass ribboned with a yellowish paste tinted with sulphur and resembling seaweed; No. 152, a small ambergris cone, with yellowish paste inlay that was welded hot and engraved. A small vase (No. 38) and a small cup approximate the natural colorations quite well, as one can see by examining the piece of amber that served as my model. These colors are in part derived from silver, as the greenish spots clearly show upon refraction in this alkaline-based glass.

Another small vase (No. 138) which is on display in the large gallery, is made of a vitreous material that is remarkable for its new and unique coloration: a yellow glass opacified with brilliant orange spots that dissolve into a greenish or bluish brown. This material acquired its iridescence in the glory hole; there it took on a pale violet-blue reflection derived from the metal in the composition.

The superimposition of pink gold on yellows that are marbled with silver produces results that, while far from natural, in no way lack for richness or surprise (see pieces No. 4, 22).

Various Colorations
I must draw to your attention an opaque glass in an antique green color that is derived from chromium and which I have used in triple and quadruple pieces. The effects of this glass are particularly remarkable in item No. 108, a kind of large cameo in which the thick brown surface layer is deeply engraved: it reveals a partial ground of antique green with plants and animals in high relief.

A cone-shaped vase (No. 139) reveals in turn, below its brown coat, a glass that has been enameled with a flaming orange color (antimonial lead) and glazed in brilliant ruby (copper). A thin layer of brown that has been left on the copper-red gives this vase its interesting smoky appearance.

Iridescent Bubbles
Items No. 99, 42, and 153 offer decorative applications of the singular handiwork I have described above. In bowl No. 99, my composition No. 81 produced bubbles in the material with a silvery-brown reflection that makes the petals of a fanciful orchid bristle with sparkling verrucae.

In No. 42, a number of elongated bubbles imitate the bubbling of water. Other bubbles splash fine drops of rain on a long-necked phial; these are due to the various compositions in which you will recognize the presence of silver.

It is silver again that allowed me the effects of certain antique types of glass that have been altered in their composition by atmospheric agents. The two-toned nuances of purple of Cassius, that vary according to the composition of the glass, have created on some pieces opaque orange spots with a certain flash to them, yellow in their reflection and crimson in transparency. I have made use of these effects on several different pieces. For the moment I note just one: a cone-shaped vase (No. 134) where the gold precipitate has marked the sodium-based glass with spots of blue, violet, currant-red, chestnut brown and earthy brown; this effect is meant to imitate the colors of the scales and petals that curl about the buds and blossoms of the magnolia.

Luster Effects (Flambé Glazing) with Copper

Items No. 19 and 25 were covered with a copper composition exposed to the gas of the glory hole. The coloration is uneven and quite varied; in some places it is hardly perceptible and occasionally appears in the form of brown traces. Bowl No. 25 was exposed to deoxidizing carbon gases and consequently assumed a flamboyant coloration. The copper appears translucent here, red upon reflection and indigo-blue upon refraction.

In the reverse case of No. 19–a vase with a rounded jade body and a yellow neck with blood-red tints–the copper on the neck, which was subjected to an oxidizing atmosphere in various successive firings, took on an initial red coloring that eventually disappeared almost altogether.

Finally, in several recent experiments, Nos. 10 and 31, a new kind of operation made a red flux appear against dark backgrounds; this technique seems to offer both glass and crystal the intensity of copper colorations that can be found in flambé glazes on porcelain.

The Imitation of Jades

The nuances of jade have inspired several colors in my work, notably potassium-sulfate alabasters, gently tinged with green by means of varying proportions of potassium bichromate and iron and copper oxides. It is important that the green shading remain very understated; otherwise it risks turning into the ordinary colors of "pressware." Nevertheless, in order to imitate imperial jade green, one may give added emphasis to it; above all it is the introduction of various colored compositions into the glass that provides the best results. As the semi-opacity of alabaster manages totally to cover up the materials that are introduced into it, it is preferable, instead of "kneading" the mixture, to apply the marbling superficially; if those effects appear too lifeless, it is better to glaze the marbling, as it were, with a layer of colorless glass. Nos. 19 and 25 offer interesting examples of this procedure.

Moss Agates and Arborized Agates

I have produced numerous applications of these white or slightly greenish crystals. Special heated preparations are incorporated and arranged during the glasswork into spotted, sandy, or speckled effects or into elegant ramifications that are joined together by the craftsman. These effects may be simple or combined, superimposed or even interlaced with layers of opaline crystal that has a small amount of white or faintly colored opacifiers.

The Museum of Decorative Arts in Paris contains a basin manufactured by me that is decorated with water-buttercups sculpted in relief on an opal layer resembling virgin wax. I have also colored opaque layers with pink gold, sometimes quite bright, at other times extremely pale (hydrangea flowers, vase 143; amaryllis flowers, vase 115); this gave me the means to express the tender nuances and the supple *morbidezza* of petals and flesh: for example, Nos. 110 and 111, a pair of covered urns. One of them takes as its motif a study of begonias, raised with a spindle in thick crimson-pink paste on a mat ash-blue ground; the other displays a cascade of semi-transparent fuschias with etched leaves in vivid shades of sharp, fresh green. Finally, item No. 116 is a bowl in the agate style with black ribbons that border on shades of green; flesh-colored flowers in the suavest of hues are cut in relief. There is also a bowl with a limpid, transparent, crystal foot of white that reveals mossy plants; the outside is enveloped, as it were, by a flight of may-flies, etched in checkered relief into a pink paste (No. 33).

Onyx-Agates: Kneaded Mixtures, Incrustations, Inner Decoration

It seems hard for me to finish, Gentlemen. And yet I must still draw your kind attention to the pleasing effects that can be created when colored ribbons are incorporated into a diaphanous mass of glass. The two vases in entry No. 53 are made with a crystal that is lightly opacified by lime phosphate into which the glassmaker has mixed ribbons of black glass before beginning his work. The designs have infinite variety; one needs only a little imagination in order to highlight them by emphasizing their form with a lightly traced sketch on the surface of the vase. One must however be careful to avoid excesses of manganese in the composition of black glass; otherwise the opalescent blue hues of the lime phosphate are affected by a common shading.

Yet another type of decoration in the mass is evident in vase No. 44, a vase made of potassium glass, tinted with copper, iron, and iridium. Fine pieces of broken glass in white enamel, shaped into butterfly wings, are gathered around one gob. The entire work is overlaid with a cap of similar material, and an application of etched motifs completes the work. A huge opaque red flower (copper protoxide), with its pistils and stamens, is enclosed in the mass of vase No. 136; the engraver had only to emphasize these effects in relief on the outside and eliminate the seams. No. 131 was also decorated literally in the mass so as to frame a preconceived subject–the inspiration that guided the fabrication of the vase by the glassmaker. In it, one can see traces of leaves, branches, and acorns, motifs that are described with an agility that rivals that of the paintbrush.

II

The Extension of My Techniques for Enriching Crystal with Enamel and Paint

Since 1878, Gentlemen, I have devoted myself continually to developing a palette that would allow me to decorate glass with the aid of colors and low-temperature vitrifiable enamels that could come close to the soft texture of heated glass. Painted and enamel decoration lack neither impressiveness nor charm. They have long been an important factor in the industrial success of our foreign competitors.

I offered you in 1878 Japanese-style enamels in relief applied to glass; at that time you predicted a promising future for this technique. Following the success of their distribution, I tried to do something new with these enamels by introducing shades that had not yet been used: different shades of blues, greens, and yellows of all kinds, including delicate and muted tones. The palettes of my enameling studios were already quite complete at the time of the Exhibition of Decorative Arts in 1884. They allowed for just about every means of decorating glass: grisaille work on small panes of glass that were applied to vases flecked with silver and gold, black cameos, yellow tinting done with silver, platinum, and gold paint, the decorative overlay of excipients with crystal colors, Bohemian white enamel, and frits of stannic acid, silex, and minium, with a dry aspect that is especially good for the adaptation of antique styles. I also developed reflecting colors by mixing them with hard Arabian enamels. Finally, in 1884, I produced for the *Union centrale* of decorative arts a new series of transparent enamels in relief.

The practice of such a large number of diverse preparations and the constant need to renew the appearance of my products led me, after my efforts were rewarded by the *Union centrale,* to explore still more innovations. I therefore present you today with the results of my continued research: opaque enamels with artificial and bizarre colors, muted nuances designed to add some "spice" to an already impressive array of colors. You will note the opaque enamels colored with gold preparations that produce pinks and lilacs that lend themselves to equally interesting work.

In short I might say that today there hardly exists a shade, however fleeting, that my palette of enamels in glass relief does not reflect, from oranges and sealing-wax red right up to violets and purples. Certain borders (see smoky quartz-type vase, No. 119 and antique box No. 147) have the delicate tones of cashmere. The glaze on these compositions is perfect, and their adhesiveness complete. Finally, the surface of these enamels may be decorated with tender colors and metallic foils that are fixed with a flux.

My entries in Class 19 and in the vestibule of honor offer varied samples of these techniques; several have even taken the full range of enamels all at once, fired at temperatures of different intensity.

New Translucent Enamels

My report to the jury of the *Union centrale* on my submissions in 1884 indicated several translucent enamels, new at the time, that were distinct from the enamels used in stained-glass work, like the beautiful, limpid blue enamel of the Arabs. Since that time, experiments in the same genre have taken place in the decoration of goblets abroad, particularly in Silesia in the factory of M. Hekkart. These preparations, with their distinctive country-fair appearance, were, however, decidedly inferior and had no relief quality to speak of. What I offer you at this time, on the other hand, are very clean enamels that possess qualities of both clarity and relief which add to their seductive appeal but also compound the difficulties inherent in their successful execution. The advantage of these translucent enamels, which are adaptable to pieces that have been previously decorated with opaque enamels, fired to a hard texture, is that they offer complete satisfaction to the eye, whether the pieces are examined in reflected or against refracted beams of light. Thus, a certain night lamp in which opaque enamel alone would have produced successful decorative effects only by daylight—a contradiction of its purpose, to be sure—can, thanks to the admixture of these colored fluxes, shine in artificial light with all the sparkle of rubies and diamonds.

Jeweled Enamels (Emaux-Bijoux)

This application led me to another. I offer you, Gentlemen, an entirely new decorative use for these low-fired enamels: a totally new series of translucent enamels that I call "jeweled enamels." My studios apply them at low temperature to a metallic foil that is fixed to my vases in a preliminary firing. The problem was to find a composition that would not alter the gilding and that was sufficiently diaphanous not to obscure the fiery metallic reflections. You see for yourselves that this small problem is resolved not without effort, for the extreme fusibility of these preparations renders their application very delicate. They must be glazed just to the point that ensures their transparency; and yet their fluidity at the muffle's low temperature can cause serious flaws. On the sides of pieces that are somewhat larger, they are exposed to even greater risks: the least unevenness of temperature is enough to drown out the ornamentation at the bottom while the ornaments at the top remain insufficiently baked. Here, nevertheless, are several important pieces on which plant motifs in emerald, topaz, amber, and ruby are clearly articulated: vases No. 270, 271, 272; platters No. 58; box No. 55.

The combination of these enamels with those previously described allowed me to imitate nature and to give to a single piece – to the winged back of a scarab or the eyes of a dragonfly – a steely blue sheen; similarly I was able to impart to an uplifted wing the diaphanous texture of living tissue and sometimes even the transparent beauty of dewdrops (No. 82).

My enamel-jewels are also of specific interest, Gentlemen, for the decoration of crystal handles and rings. On principle, no doubt, the simulation of another art is to be discouraged. Nevertheless, I decided that by decorating and enriching such fragile bands with the ornaments of a jeweler, the effect for the eye was particularly pleasing. I have, however, discreetly limited my use of this technique (goblets and carafes of the rock crystal type).

Champlevé Enamels
One of my techniques comes very close to that of champlevé enamels on copper and to the sixteenth-century technique of incrustations on rock crystal (bowl No. 21, vase No. 39, seal No. 286, goblet No. 289). Grooved areas were etched in the glass and then gilded in the oven. They then received as many firings with the translucent enamel as necessary, until their surface was perfectly flush with that of the piece.

Low-temperature Underlaid Decorations
I must also mention what I have called low-temperature underlaid decorations, borrowing this term from faience painters. These are very fusible glazes that are adapted to the hard glass that must take them; they glaze it with odd patinas (vases No. 273, 89, and 233 to 236), by saturating the misty clouds and the landscapes in cameo with a vitreous flux that is colored with etchings. No. 278, called "mosaic work," is an example of this type.

Trapped Glass
By way of conclusion to Part II of my note, I would like to point out to you the doubled glass (Nos. 286 to 288) that is quite distinct from the doubled glass produced in Bohemia in the seventeenth and eighteenth centuries: this by virtue of its large dimensions and by the fact that the decoration which is enclosed within it while hot, itself undergoes several firings. The capsule contained on the inside, which is indistinguishable from the outer capsule, was decorated with encrusted enamel-jewels; it was then inserted into the outer capsule whose seam is entirely covered with opaque enamel decoration.

III

Additional Tools for the Crystal Engraver. The Development and Application of Different Means and Techniques for Engraving Crystal. Works of Art
In order to produce some of the engraved works that my factory presents to you here, Gentlemen, I had to develop special tools which I use for refining rough materials. The well-known hardness of certain potassium-base glasses, as well as the need to hollow out ornaments from below, led me to invent a vertical shaping spindle, designed especially for the deep carving of massive crystal. It is in techniques such as this, no doubt, that one must look for an explanation of the kind of work done in the Far East in the seventeenth century, pieces treated by the Chinese in the manner of ivory; their surprising technique may one day be the object of a written contribution by me to the already rich history of glass.

The simultaneous practice of all the techniques of engraving on crystal – from wheel engraving and, – if I may coin the phrase, – spindle-sculpting, right up to acid baths and diamond-point engraving – offers you in the presentation of my work an extremely diversified picture of this art. For the engraving of my work, I have made use of all the resources available: patinas, both lustrous and matte, soft textures that are pleasing to the eye and the touch, bas-reliefs, cameos, foregrounds embossed in the round, and backgrounds with a stained glass effect, with lithophanic reliefs that are carved with spindles of the finest dimension. You will find such an example in the work on the large vase, No. 68 (Joan of Arc). Here the opaque cameo engraving of the foreground surface moves into stained glass work in the deeper surfaces, in such a way that the work remains of interest both in its refraction and reflection of light.

The Uses of Hydrofluoric Acid
This was of no use to me at all in the actual engraving, because, as I shall soon explain, I never apply the precious elaboration of masses in relief onto the private depths of that mysterious background which alone provides the charm of the tooling – that is, the sweet accompaniment, the animated dialog between a sculpted motif and the material substance from which it blossoms.

To be sure, had the acid been able to help me speed up the laborious deliberation of etching motifs, of isolating them and carving out the hollows of the background, I would certainly not have hesitated to make use thereof. But the definitive value of art appreciates in terms of the final result. My own work bears upon the alteration of materials that play off the lamination of superimposed layers of density, composition, and varied thicknesses. Of these the craftsman can have no knowledge before he penetrates the substance with his tool. Thus it is that the most insignificant gesture, etched blindly by a careless hand, can spoil everything; nothing replaces the hand of an artist who knows exactly what he wants.

While acid cannot think, cannot shape, or finish, it can nonetheless sculpt; it cuts into certain kinds of glass in a special way that is all its own. I have made use of these aggressive etchings to produce ornamentation with a decidedly archaic character, to scrape away surfaces in which I wished to emphasize a natural rather than a fabricated effect. Thus, on vase No. 68, the ancient spear-head ornaments were first carved into shape and then scoured and eaten away by acid.

A satisfying use of this technique can be found in fine, fragile ornaments that are point-engraved in a protective varnish and then hollowed out with acid. The result resembles the delicate precision of lacework; the exact detail fades out in a way that no other technique can possibly match. These designs are covered with grisaille work and serve as the ground for motifs that are emphasized in the front. In this vein, I draw your attention to a jewel case and to the goblets that appear woven and embroidered; also, an enormous night lamp that looks like it has been covered with a sheer, black silk veil, embroidered with Arabic-French characters in translucent blue enamel and mat gold that spell out: "Through all troubles hope shines within me."

Acid reaches easily into those areas that the spindle cannot touch. At the *Union centrale* of decorative arts, I displayed some vases with decorative grounds that had been applied on the inner side; I was thus able to represent both vapors and the cellular tissue of petals and leaves.

An ornamental design traced with diamond and then gilded over also decorates a large, peacock-blue covered jar, with this motto in Zend, followed by a translation: "Good words, good thoughts, good actions."

How I Have Interpreted Crystal Engraving
You are no doubt familiar, Gentlemen, with skillful examples of engraving where the crystal, beautiful as it may be in itself, is overwhelmed, as it were, beneath the weight of such long, meticulous handiwork—work that seems unconscious of time, of the object, and of life itself. It is almost as if one had forgotten to turn off a magical machine that robot-like engravers use to create the lasting, impeccable, and imperturbable

sculpture of cold masterpieces. "Admirable workers," exclaims M. Bonnaffé, "as remarkable to be sure as the galley-slave who carves a fully rigged ship out of a coconut with the tip of his pocketknife." "Cold, hard objects," responds in turn M. Eugène Guillaume, with reference to certain engravings on precious stones, "like those produced by Jeuffroy at the turn of this century. They express only the boredom of the artist and the difficulties that the practice of his profession set in his way."

In keeping with the noble lessons of these masters of French art, I have found in engraving above all a means of expression, a means to bring forth out of warm and living material all the elements that have been consolidated within it. Even in those pieces that took longest to elaborate, I never forgot the need for moderation: the enthusiasms of the artist must not suffocate the material from which he composes his work.

I would hope therefore that you might discover in the materials that I set before you and in the execution of the hand, all the *flaws*—this sooner than silence, than dryness of execution, than mere love of prettiness, than the monotony of technique or the impression of boredom! In order to avoid the appearance of mechanical work, we have therefore been more casual in the description of accessory detail: we have concentrated all our attention on one given point. In the presentation of a harvest of fine, ripened fruit, one sees the side of the sun just out of focus. We have sought to avoid the appearance of stamped impressions, of molds, and of reproductions; we have let the contours of our engravings flow into the background. Our tools have marked their form in crystal, and with that form marked, too, all the tenderness and respect of the craftsman for his material.

If one were to make plaster molds of my engraved works, stripped of their color and soft relief, there would remain, no doubt, very little to speak of; nevertheless, it would be clear that these were crystals and not bronzes or ivories.

IV

Industrial Applications. Artistic Vulgarization
In submitting to you, after my refined objects of luxury, samples of my manufacture that are adapted to more modest needs, I do not feel that I have moved down a grade. Neither my workers nor I have found it impossible to reconcile affordable production and art; we have not judged the commercial dressing of crystal to be necessarily a mark of poor taste. The Orient, uninfluenced by the prejudices of the West, has managed to produce stunning merchandise with infinite art. Sufficient manpower,—but no excess of person-

nel—well-trained and conscientious, an adequate supply of tools and especially models, a technical practice that is rich in craftsmanship and means, and a studio for design and artistic applications that directs the work: these are the conditions that have allowed me to provide goods to our retail merchants and exporters at a modest price.

I have not been content to produce masterful objects alone; I have also striven to make art accessible so as to open a less restricted number of minds to works that are more complex. I have propagated the feeling of nature, of the grace of flowers, and the beauty of insects. My work over the past twenty-four years has already given birth to a considerable body of shapes, styles, ideas and infinitely varied genres in the imaginative fabrication of glass. I therefore present myself to you proudly as a vulgarizer of art.

You will find among my works the proof that neither art nor taste need depend on costly means; that the producer need only guard his personal sense of grace, and he can submit his models and decorations to economic reason and the practical details of his craft.

In my low-cost production, I have avoided all that is artificial, extravagant, and fragile. I have used solid colorations. Endless creations have influenced the taste of the average public. In the factory I have opened and paved the way—sometimes to my own detriment—for the profitable mass production of crystal. There have been imitations of "Gallé-type" glass; all I can say is that I am pleased.

I may only wish that moderation, temperance, and good taste always preside over the use that is made elsewhere of my humble discoveries! And may those discoveries benefit from an increased esteem for the material that is dear to us rather than inflate the inventory of a debased and discredited line of production.

V

The Organization of a Special Studio for the Decorative Composition of Crystal; Material Ruled by Art
I have created at my factory a special studio of composition and design for glass production. Placed under my immediate supervision, this studio generates the work for all the others.

Here the profiles are drawn for the manufacture of the wooden forms designed for glassblowing; from here also come the watercolors and cartoons for the enamelers, engravers and painters. Many models of natural and still life are placed at the disposal of the studio, thanks to the gardens and to the collection of natural history at the factory.

My own work consists above all in the execution of personal dreams: to dress crystal in tender and terrible roles, to compose for it the thoughtful faces of pleasure or tragedy, to assemble all the elements and carefully prepare the effective production of my future projects, to order technique in the service of preconceived works of art, and to weigh the operational scale of chance with possibilities for success at the time of the decisive operation, once called the master-work. In other words, insofar as I am capable, from the start, I impose upon the changeable and changing material at my disposal the suitable qualities I should like it to have—the material and its colorations, the material and its measures—in order to incarnate my dream and my design.

Needless to say, all of these calculations can be, and often are, disrupted by unforeseen causes; but the very hazards of a craft in which fire collaborates, violently and brutally, often serve me in the most fortuitous way.

Sometimes, in fact, I enjoy playing with the products of accidents that then become the objects of teasing challenges—baroque little problems that the motley material sets before my imagination. In just such a way, the prolonged gaze of the invalid transforms the marblings of wallpaper into thousands of strange figures, or the clouds at twilight appear to a child like immense sheep folds, while the sailor's eye sees in them rolling whitecaps and beaches.

It is through a similar process that engravers of hard gems—like Soldi, Lemaire, and Schultz—have managed to avail themselves of the strange designs of onyx and ribboned agate: "What charm this art has!" remarks M. Eugène Guillaume, in the *Studies of Art and Nature,* which this eminent professor at the Collège de France has recently collected in a single volume devoted to ancient and modern art—"What charm this art has! To take a gem as nature has made it, complete with irregularities and capricious designs; to profit from the varied colors that enrich it in order to distinguish within a composition nudes, draperies, or accessories; to follow the nuances of color in the reduction in thickness of the layers that constitute it; to become for a moment a slave to matter in order to force it to express an idea, and to make nature play her game so that the final work may seem the result of a preconceived agreement between chance and the genius of an engraver: this is the kind of work that solicits all the spirit of invention, all the resources and all the skill of an artist."

This, Gentlemen, is indeed a seductive art. And yet these masters themselves would envy the power that glassmakers possess to form with their own hands agates and marbles.

It has caught my fancy to work with awesome onyxes and to wrap a vase in streams of lava and pitch; to enlist the Styx and the Acheron Rivers on the foot of a bowl, to use a flaming meteor and the gases of hell to separate Orpheus from Eurydice who lies faint in a sooty brown crystal.

As I have written under one of my vases, I sow burning flames and then gather up with my spindle paradoxical blossoms from the depths of the dark layers where I know they lie waiting. Is it not for us that the poet has written:
    I harvest in secret mysterious flowers!

How then could I have consented to place my art under the tutelage of unconscious matter, made to obey the scepter of the glassmaker, the magic wand of the sorcerer who holds it enslaved to his fancy? Thus it is, Gentlemen, that I am not only responsible for the uses that can be made of crystal but also for the point of departure in this adventure. I have sought to make crystal yield forth all the tender or fierce expression it can summon when guided by a hand that delights in it. And it is I who have infused it, as it were, with the means for touching us: the worrisome blackness or the delicate *morbidezza* of soft rose petals.

VI

French Crystal Enters into Art Collections
and Collections of Curiosities with
Modern Style and Sentiment

Gentlemen, so many varied preoccupations would never have succeeded entirely in conquering your sympathy if, in my work, I had limited myself to the application of ready-made decorations, conceived for other materials; decorations that had their source everywhere except in a deep personal conviction—even in archeological reconstitutions, in variations of pieces that our ancestors, the glassmakers, had bequeathed to us.

People complain that the admiration of ancient objects of art is exclusive, that it has persisted too long and stifled new incentives. It has been my belief that the production of works that are modern in conception and French in their syntax might better restore our esteem than all the sterile complaints. I have sought to make objects that would seem one day to have lived in their own time, that is our own.

It must, however, be admitted that the extraordinary perfection of French crystal in earlier days failed to touch the limited group that then dominated the world of art, the refined public, subtle, erudite, even eclectic, entranced by mystery, but scornful nonetheless of correct and mechanical execution, infinitely blasé and for this reason enamored of naïveté, moved by ingenuous expression!

The present experiments have been favorably received. I do not mean to suggest that I alone am responsible for this. In fact I have not been the only man to open up to modern French crystal the doors of the museums and those of the no less inaccesible private collections, exclusive doors that until now have been only half-open to the products of Venice, Bohemia, or Arabian glass, and to the exquisite crystals of the Far East.

It is, however, with pleasure, Gentlemen, that you may one day note that in 1889 a glorious threshold, long closed to the arts that ennoble useful objects, was finally opened wide before the youthful finery of French crystal.

TRANSLATED BY SIMA GODFREY

BIBLIOGRAPHY

Those seeking detailed bibliographic information about Gallé and his period are referred to the excellent compilations in *Nancy 1900...* (see Munich. Stadtmuseum) and Bernd Hakenjos' published doctoral dissertation. Charpentier has made a useful study of the earliest biographies of Gallé in "Remarques sur les premières biographies de Gallé parues de son temps." Readers seeking biographies in English should consult Garner, *Emile Gallé;* the sections in Bloch-Dermant, *The Art of French Glass 1860-1914;* and Ada Polak, *Modern Glass.* An English translation of Gallé's *Ecrits pour l'Art* is available in the library of The Corning Museum of Glass, as are many of the items listed below.

ARNOLD, D. L. "Art Glass of Gallé." *Western Collector* 5, No. 6, June 1967, pp. 6-12.

ARWAS, VICTOR. *Glass: Art Nouveau to Art Deco.* New York: Rizzoli, 1977, p. 84.

BARRELET, JAMES. *La verrerie en France de l'èpoque Gallo-Romaine à nos jours.* Paris: Librarie Larousse, 1953.

BARTEN, SIGRID. "Glas von Emile Gallé: Arbeiten eines Art Nouveau-Künstlers in schweizer Sammlungen." *Weltkunst* 50, No. 11, June 1, 1980, pp. 1568-1570.

BLOCH-DERMANT, JANINE. *The Art of French Glass 1860-1914.* New York: The Vendome Press, 1980.

_____. "Le décor floral des verreries d'Emile Gallé, création et évolution." *L'Estampille,* No. 104, Dec. 1978, pp. 16-27.

_____. "Emile Gallé et la marqueterie de verre." *L'Estampille,* No. 108, April 1979, pp. 8-17.

BLOUNT, BERNIECE and HENRY. *French Cameo Glass.* Des Moines, Iowa: authors, 1968.

BOUR, EMILE. "Emile Gallé." *La Lorraine artiste* 23, No. 1, January 1905, pp. 3-15.

BRIARD, EMMANUEL. "Nécrologie: Emile Gallé." *Bulletin des sociétés artistiques de l'est,* 1904, pp. 154-161.

CANTELLI, GIUSEPPE. "Emile Gallé." *Antichità Viva* 6, No. 6, 1967, pp. 29-37.

CHARPENTIER, FRANÇOISE-THÉRÈSE. "L'Art de Gallé a-t-il été influencé par Baudelaire?" *Gazette des beaux-arts* 61, (N.S.) Nos. 1132-1133, May-June 1963, pp. 367-374.

_____. "Ascendance lorraine de Gallé." *Le Pays Lorrain* 56, 1975, pp. 153-157.

_____. "Du pastiche à l'Art Nouveau la demeure d'Emile Gallé à Nancy, 1874-1904." In *Situazione degli studi sul Liberty: Atti del convegno internazionale.* Florence: Clusf, 1976, pp. 207-208.

_____. "L'Ecole de Nancy." *Jardin des arts* 73, 1960, pp. 23-33.

_____. *Emile Gallé.* Nancy: Université de Nancy II, 1978.

_____. "Quelques sources de décor des verriers Lorrains entre 1867 et 1900." In *VIIᵉ Congrès International du Verre: Comptes Rendus.* Marcinelle, Belgium: Maison d'Edition, 1965, Vol. 2, paper 210, 5 pp.

_____. "Remarques sur les premières biographies de Gallé parues de son temps." In *A Travers l'art français: du moyen âge au XXᵉ siècle.* Paris: F. DeNobele, 1978, pp. 419-429, chart.

CHOUX, JACQUES. "F.-Th. Charpentier, *Emile Gallé,* Nancy 1978." *Annales de l'est* (Series 5) 31, No. 2, 1979, pp. 172-174. [Book Review]

DEMORIANE, HÉLÈNE. "Le cas étrange de Monsieur Gallé." *Connaissance des arts,* No. 102, August 1960, pp. 34-41.

DENNIS, RICHARD. "The Glass of Emile Gallé." In Wilson, Peter (Ed.), *Antiques International: Collector's Guide to Current Trends.* New York: Putnam, 1967, pp. 182-192.

DESJARDINS, PAUL. "Un Lorrain à l'exposition: Oeuvre de Emile Gallé." *La Lorraine Artiste* 7, No. 34, Sept. 3, 1889, pp. 529-531. (Reprint from *Journal des debats* 1889.)

DUNCAN, ALASTAIR and DE BARTHA, GEORGES. *Glass by Gallé.* London: Thames and Hudson, 1984.

DURET-ROBERT, FRANÇOIS. "Ecole de Nancy: Gallé." *Connaissance des arts,* No. 232, June 1971, pp. 67-70; No. 234, Aug. 1971, pp. 19, 20; No. 239, Jan. 1972, pp. 23-26.

EMILE GALLÉ: N. EL FITURI COLLECTION. Text by Philippe Garner. Lausanne: Heliographia, 1982, 84 pp.

FABER-CASTELL, CHRISTIAN VON. "Vier falsche Gallé-Vasen: Experten decken Jugendstil-Fälshungen auf." *Weltkunst* 53, No. 12, June 15, 1983, pp. 1644-1647.

FOURCAUD, LOUIS DE. *Emile Gallé.* Paris: Librairie de l'art ancien et moderne, 1903.

FRANTZ, HENRI. "Emile Gallé and the Decorative Artists of Nancy." *The Studio* 28, 1903, pp. 108-117.

FUCHS, L. F. "Der Glaskünstler Emile Gallé." *Die Weltkunst* 31, No. 19, Oct. 1, 1961, p. 17.

GALERIE MANZI, JOYANT. *Catalogue des Objets d'Art Moderne...Faisant partie de la Collection Roger Marx.* Paris: The Gallery, 1914. "Gallé," Items 64-106.

GALLÉ, EMILE. *Ecrits pour l'art: floriculture, art décoratif, notices d'exposition 1884-1889.* Ed. Henriette Gallé-Grimm. Paris: Librairie Renouard, 1908. (Reprint: Marseille: Laffitte Reprints, 1980)

GARNER, PHILIPPE. "Emile Gallé en sa cristallerie à Nancy. Symbolist und Kunsthandwerker." *Weltkunst,* No. 23, Dec. 1, 1975, p. 2282-2283.

_____. *Emile Gallé.* New York: Rizzoli, 1976.

_____. *Glass 1900: Gallé, Tiffany, Lalique.* London: Thames & Hudson, 1979.

GILLET, LOUIS. "Emile Gallé: Le poème du verre." *Revue Hébdomadaire* 19, 1910, pp. 153-172.

GROS, GABRIELLA. "Poetry in Glass: The Art of Emile Gallé 1846-1905." *Apollo* 62, Nov. 1955, pp. 134-136.

GROVER, RAY and LEE. *Art Glass Nouveau.* Rutland, Vt.: Charles E. Tuttle, 1967, pp. 184, 190f.

_____. *Carved and Decorated European Art Glass.* Rutland, Vt.: Charles E. Tuttle, 1970.

HAKENJOS, BERND. *Emile Gallé: Keramik, Glas und Möbel des Art Nouveau.* (Inaugural-Dissertation), Cologne: Universität zu Köln, 1982.

HANNOVER, EMIL. "Emile Gallé." *Kunst und Künstler* 3, 1905, pp. 290-297.

_____. "Emile Gallés Glas." *Tidsskrift for Kunstindustri* 5, 1889, pp. 192-197.

HENRIVAUX, JULES. "Emile Gallé." *L'Art Décoratif* 7, 1905 (78), pp. 124-135.

_____. "La verrerie à l'Exposition universelle de 1889." *Revue des arts décoratifs* 10, No. 6, Dec. 1889, pp. 174, 177-184.

_____. *La verrerie au XXe siècle.* Paris: L. Geisler, 1911.

_____. *Le verre et le cristal.* (Encyclopédia chimique, tome V, Applications de chimie inorganique, 5e fasc.) Paris: Dunod, 1883.

HILSCHENZ, HELGA. *Das Glas des Jugendstils: Katalog der Sammlung Hentrich im Kunstmuseum Düsseldorf.* (Materialien zur Kunst des 19. Jahrhunderts, Band 8) Munich: Prestel-Verlag, 1973.

HINZELIN, EMILE. "Emile Gallé." *La Lorraine Artiste* 23, 1905, pp. 16-21.

HOFMANN, HELGA. "Gallé avant Gallé." In *Festchrift Luitpold Dussler.* Munich: Deutscher Kunstverlag, 1972, pp. 433-456.

JAPONISME: JAPANESE INFLUENCE ON FRENCH ART, 1854-1910. (Exhibition catalog) Cleveland: Cleveland Museum of Art, (1975).

KLESSE, BRIGITTE. "Meisenthal oder Nancy? Addenda zu Emile Gallé." *Sonderdruck aus dem Wallraf-Richartz-Jahrbuch. Band XLII.* Cologne: Dumont Buchverlag, 1981. (Also issued as text of exhibition catalog: *Auf den kunstlerischen Spuren Emile Gallés.* Cologne: Kunstgewerbemuseum, 1982).

LANORVILLE, G. "Les cristaux d'art d'Emile Gallé." *La Nature, Rev. des sciences et de leurs applications aux arts et à l'industrie* 36, No. 2075, March 1, 1913, pp. 209-212.

LAURENT, MARCEL. "Un livre d'Emile Gallé: 'Ecrits pour l'art.'" *La Vie actuelle,* No. 4, April 1909 12 pp.

MALMÖ. MALMÖ MUSEUM. *Emile Gallé: En glaskonstens mästare.* (Exhibition catalog) Malmö: The Museum, 1966.

MARX, ROGER. "Emile Gallé au Salon de 1891." *La Lorraine Artiste* 9, Sept. 20, 1891, pp. 600-601.

_____. "Emile Gallé: Psychologie de l'artiste et synthèse de l'oeuvre." *Art et décoration* 30, No. 8, August 1911, pp. 231-252.

_____. *La Décoration et l'art industriel à l'Exposition universelle en 1889.* Paris: Librairies-Imprimeries Réunies, 1890.

_____. "La décoration architecturale et les industries d'art a l'Exposition universelle de 1889." *Revue des arts décoratifs* 11, 1890/91, pp. 32-41.

_____. "Les précurseurs. I: Conférence sur Emile Gallé." In *L'Art social: Exemples et réalisations,* Paris: 1913, pp. 111-151.

MEIXMORON DE DOMBASLE, CHARLES DE. "Réponse du Président M. Ch. de Meixmoron de Dombasle au Récipiendaire M. Emile Gallé. Academie de Stanislas, Séance solanelle 17.5.1900." *Mémories de l'Académie de Stanislas,* Nancy 1899/1900, pp. 1-25.

MICHEL, FRANÇOIS. "Les fleurs mystérieuses d'Emile Gallé." *Gazette médicale de France* 77, No. 33, Dec. 15, 1970, pp. 7735-7737.

MONTESQUIOU, COMTE ROBERT DE. "Les verres forgés." Exposition d'Emile Gallé au Musée Galliéra. *Les Arts,* No. 106, Oct. 1910, pp. 30-32.

MUNICH. STADTMUSEUM. *Nancy 1900-Jugendstil in Lothringen zwischen Historismus und Art Deco/1865-1930,*

Mainz: Münchner Stadtmuseum, 1980.

NICHOLAS, EMILE. "Emile Gallé à l'Exposition 1900." *La Lorraine Artiste* 18, No. 8, Nov. 1, 1900, pp. 113-115.

NIHON-KEIZI SHIMBUN, Tokyo. *Emile Gallé: Exposition.* Tokyo: Nihon-Keizai Shimbun, 1980. (In Japanese with English titles)

O'NEAL, WILLIAM B. "Three Art Nouveau Glass Makers." *Journal of Glass Studies* 2, 1960, pp. 125-137.

OWSLEY, DAVID T. "Emile Gallé: Poet in Glass." *Carnegie Magazine* 45, No. 4, April 1971, pp. 141-144.

PAGUY, RAYMOND. "Les Poèmes vitrifiés d'Emile Gallé." *ABC Décor,* No. 74/75, Dec. 1970– Jan. 1971, pp. 96f.

PAZAUREK, GUSTAV E. "Emile Gallé." *Mitteilungen des nordböhmischen Gewerbemuseums* 22, No. 3, 1904, pp. 75-79.

_____. *Moderne Gläser.* Leipzig: Hermann Seemann Nachfolger, [1902].

POLAK, ADA. "Background to Gallé." In *Annales du 4e Congrès des Journées Internationales du Verre, Ravenne-Venise 13-20. May 1967.* Liège: Association International pour l'Histoire du Verre, 1967, pp. 206-213.

_____. "Gallé Glass: Luxurious, Cheap and Imitated." *Journal of Glass Studies* 5, 1963, pp. 105-115.

_____. "A Great Glassmaker: The Idealistic Art of Emile Gallé." *The Antique Dealer and Collectors' Guide* 16, No. 3 (NS) Oct. 1961, p. 29ff.

_____. *Modern Glass.* London: Faber and Faber, 1962.

_____. "Signatures on Gallé Glass." *Journal of Glass Studies* 8, 1966, pp. 120-123.

RICE, WILLIAM MARSH, University, Houston, Texas, Institute for the Arts. *Art Nouveau: Belgium/France: Catalogue of an Exhibition Organized by the Institute for the Arts, Rice University, and The Art Institute of Chicago.* Ed. Yvonne Brunhammer et al. Houston: Rice University, 1976, pp. 212-225; No. 318-344, p. 475f.

RUDDER, JEAN-LUC DE. "Les Poèmes vitrifiés d'Emille Gallé." *L'Estampille,* No. 13, Sept. 1970, pp. 32-38, 62-63.

SCHULZE-KREFELD, PAUL. "Erstlingsarbeiten Emile Gallé." *Die Werkkunst* 2, 1905/1906, pp. 236-237.

ST., FR. "Emile Gallé–Nancy." *Deutsche Kunst und Dekoration* 15, October 1904, p. 138.

SOCIÉTÉ DES AMIS DES ARTS DE STRASBOURG. *Exposition d'art décoratif de l'Ecole de Nancy, au Palais de Rohan.* Strasbourg: Imp. Alsacienne, 1908.

THIOLERE, ED. "Les Etablissements Emile Gallé à Nancy." (Monographies Industrielles) *Société industrielle de l'Est,* No. 11, Nancy 1906, pp. 275-283.

VARENNE, GASTON. "La pensée et l'art d'Emile Gallé." *Mercure de France* 86, No. 313, 1910, pp. 31-44.

WARMUS, WILLIAM. *Emile Gallé: Dreams into Glass.* Exhibition catalog. Corning, New York: The Corning Museum of Glass, 1984.

YOSHIMIZU, TSUNEO. *Emiru Gare Sono Hito to Salcuhin.* Tokyo: Garasu Shobo, 1977.

ZURICH. MUSEUM BELLERIVE ZURICH. *Emile Gallé: Keramik, Glas und Möbel des Art Nouveau* (ed. Sigrid Barten). Zurich: the museum, 1980.